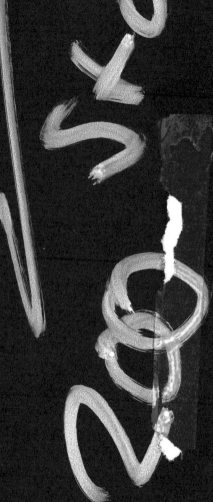

HOLGER JUNG, JEAN-REMY VON MATT
MOMENTUM
THE FORCE THAT COMMUNICATION NEEDS TODAY.

All rights reserved, especially the rights of mechanical, electronic, or photographic reproduction, storage and processing in electronic systems, reprinting in newspapers or magazines, public presentation, filming or dramatization, broadcasting via radio, television, or video, in parts or as a whole.

Original edition
1st edition March 2002
6th expanded and updated edition, December 2011
2nd English edition April 2013
Translated from German by Gerhard Schulte
© 2002 by Holger Jung and Jean-Remy von Matt

Cover photos: Giovanni Castell, Hamburg (outer cover)
                Geo and Daniel Fuchs, Neuberg (inner cover)
Design: Jung von Matt AG
Typesetting: Marion Beeck, Jung von Matt/basis GmbH
Printing: Druckerei Wagner Verlag und Werbung GmbH
Printed in Germany

ISBN 978-3-00-040821-2

www.jvm.com

PREFACE

There is a very basic change that affects advertising as we know it as well as other marketing communication tasks: people have not only become accustomed to communicating quickly and informally via digital media but also to getting themselves involved, even if it is just a comment or review. This requires campaigns that can do more than send the correct message to the correct target audience.

All of these are changes that influence our work. That is why we added an extra chapter to "Momentum." And what implies this new chapter 15? A critical review of the recommendations and expectations of the chapters preceding it.

CONTENT

INTRODUCTION 11

1 THE LEVER PRINCIPLE OF COMMUNICATION 19
   About the economic significance of great ideas

2 A GOOD HORSE HAS A TIGHT JUMP.
   GOOD ADVERTISING DOESN'T 43
   About the self-fulfilling power of ambitious goals

3 IF YOU HAVE SOMETHING IMPORTANT TO SAY,
   DON'T USE LONG SENTENCES 65
   About concentration and reduction

4 CREATIVITY PAYS.
   BUT WHICH ONE OF THE TWO? 89
   About the effect of creativity

5 SCRATCHES ARE SEXY, THE SWEAT OF FEAR ISN'T 109
   About provocation in advertising

6 WHY RIGHT ADVERTISING IS WRONG 131
   About the correlation between strategy and creativity

7 THE BEST STRATEGISTS ARE LAZY GENIUSES 155
   About those who are supposed to lead the way for the creative ones

8 THE BRAND'S JOURNEY FROM THE FLAG TO THE DRESS 175
   About images, identity, and identification

DEAR READERS!

WE HATE BAD IDEAS.
PARTICULARLY WHEN THEY COME FROM US.

That's why we try to learn as much as possible from every experience in our exciting field on a daily basis.

At some point, we decided to pass on what we have learned. To our co-workers, our customers, our students — but also to all others who invest a lot of time or money in this fascinating subject matter.

That's how this book was created. And only after a short time, Momentum became the most widely read specialty book about advertising in German, and it is currently in its 6th expanded and updated edition.

We hope you will enjoy reading this book as much as we enjoyed writing it!

Holger Jung   Jean-Remy von Matt

PREFACE

The last decade has changed communication more than the one hundred years preceding it. But "Momentum" has hardly aged since its first edition.

On the one hand, this is due to the fact that the book explicitly refers to a type of communication that is intended to conquer customers in mass markets — in other words, advertising in its purest form: vying for the customer's favor. On the other hand, the book deals with many topics that have universal validity, independent from media and usage behavior.

This includes, for example, the appeal of surprising, memorable wordings, plots or images. These phenomena do not change, even after the digitalization of the media world. On the contrary, they have become even more important.

Certain passages deal with developments that have since become reality, for example, that media consumption has become more voluntary in the digital age and thus communication ideas must be better than ever. Boredom in advertising has never been as deadly as it is today.

In retrospect, some assertions must be corrected or at least refined; for example, the warning about keeping brands from falling into the hands of "digital technicians," or the statement that the Internet would always be relegated to second tier as an advertising medium.

PREFACE

Increasingly, digital experts no longer fit the nerd cliché but they are an intelligent force that securely leads brands through the jungle of modern-day possibilities.

And the Internet has blossomed into one of the most influential mass media. In Germany, online media reach more than 50 million people. In younger markets, such as the BRIC states, their reach is slightly less pronounced in terms of the total population, but the brands can reach their most attractive target audience mainly in online venues.

The most important changes our industry has been dealing with over the past few years only partly affect the "laws" of good communication. They also result from the fact that "advertising"— in the sense of conquering a large number of new customers in a short period of time — is continuously losing significance.

This is due to the fact that it has become more lucrative in many markets to retain the customer base and build a mutually valuable relationship. And also because other forms of communication, such as digital information and service offers "on demand" or the very specific, individualized approach, are more effective and economical.

But it is also due to the fact that, although mass markets still exist, even there, the request for individualization of services is growing. And, last but not least, because the "long tail," the many small niche markets, can suddenly be quite profitable due to the presence of the Internet and new paths of conquering customers.

9 IF YOU WANT TO LEAD BRANDS TO SUCCESS,
YOU HAVE TO BE A SUCCESS YOURSELF 197
About marketing in an ad agency

10 THE TRAINING WHEELS OF MARKETING 217
About the questionable nature of opinion polls

11 PENETRATION AND PERSISTANCE:
UNEQUAL BROTHERS 241
About size in communication

12 A FIST IS STRONGER THAN FIVE FINGERS 261
About the added value of integrated concepts

13 THE PEOPLE DETERMINE WHAT BECOMES A SLOGAN 285
About good, bad, and no slogans

14 IN THE NO MAN'S LAND BETWEEN
FEELING AND KNOWING 303
About the relationship between ad agency and client

15 BOREDOM HAS NEVER BEEN AS DEADLY AS TODAY 327
About communication in the digital world

INTRODUCTION
THERE ARE RULES FOR ADVERTISING
FOR GOOD ADVERTISING, THERE ARE EXCEPTIONS

This book begins where the science of communication ends. Right in the middle of practice. With a combined track record of over 60 years on the front lines in the battle for better advertising, we would like to pass along our experiences.

For all those who spend a lot of time with advertising. For all those who invest a lot of money in advertising. Especially for those among them who have recurrent doubts about the purpose of their investment.

There is plenty of eloquence in the communication industry. A lot has already been said about how to do advertising. How to make advertising better. And most of all, why advertising is such a tough business.

ADVERTISERS HAVE BEEN COMPLAINING FOR YEARS.

Most of the experts who have recently published books agree. And paint the same sinister picture. They regret the palette of increasingly interchangeable products. They mourn the death of uniqueness.

Most of all, they lament the stiffer competition to reception and effect — the deluge of information.

INTRODUCTION

The permanent, by irritating white noise of marketing communication has turned into a collective tinnitus. And the experts prove with frightening statistics how many messages inundate the consumer on a daily basis.

A man can choose among five car brands that suit his needs and abilities. He can choose among three possible wives in his lifetime. Three times, perhaps four in special cases, he is so close to a woman that marriage becomes a topic.

His choice of profession is limited by his education and affinities. Seven professions might seriously be considered. If he goes to a restaurant, he can choose among five main courses. On his way home, between two routes.

But every day this man has to choose among 4,500 advertising messages. He must decide which one to take along and which to leave behind. From this flood of offers the experts of the ads deduce that today's advertising should be more inspiring, more creative, more courageous.

This is by no means wrong, but it is also nothing new. Because the flood of information began with Gutenberg. It has been discussed since the middle of the 20th century, when Walter Benjamin wrote "The Work of Art in the Age of Mechanical Reproduction." At a time when media sciences did not yet exist.

Perception has long since evolved. The consumer has grown accustomed to the flood and isn't drowning in it either. He didn't just learn to swim, now he surfs on the waves of information.

INTRODUCTION

He's on top of it. And uses every new wave coming towards him. He is not stressed. Above all, he is spoiled. He is not a victim. Effortlessly, he is in control of the situation and gleefully selects from all the communication offerings.

And this is where the era of "super cleaning power" ends. Advertising loses its old right to burst into our living rooms unannounced and expect a friendly reception. The future of advertising is determined by the fact that media consumption is becoming more and more voluntary. And this is a new challenge for us advertisers.

HOW DO I SEDUCE A PRIMADONNA?

How do I win over a spoiled consumer? Spoiled by more and more opportunities to get specific information. But also opportunities to escape from specific information. From remote control zapping to the "Web Washer" that eliminates ad banners from his Internet browser.

How do I win over an enlightened, emancipated, self-confident consumer? How do I win over someone who sees through me? Who won't be fooled? How do I make sure that those who purse their lips when they see advertising will smile about mine?

There is an island where the indigenous people have an odd custom. If a tree is too thick to be cut down with an axe, they scream at it. Every day for a month. Then the tree falls by itself.

INTRODUCTION

You might laugh at this custom, think it primitive. But are we highly-paid advertising experts any different? Don't we scream at the consumer until he gives in?

We kept getting louder and louder to keep our audience. We wanted to solve the problem by hitting the gas pedal. Like the driver who notices that he is low on fuel and instinctively steps on the gas to reach the nearest filling station as quickly as possible. Even though he should know that he will reach his destination more safely by slowing down a bit.

We used the arsenal of advertising to obtain stopping power. In ballistics, this term describes a weapon's ability to stop an opponent. But is this the right tool to turn strangers into friends? How long did we equate loudness with effectiveness and produce one screaming campaign after another?

How long did we think it was enough to win the

WAR FOR EYEBALLS?

We all lament the volumetime quotient that remains for today's customer to process information. We are worried about the casual reception of advertising. About turning down the volume during commercial breaks.

The consumer is still imagined to be standing gamely in front of us or even coming towards us. Actually, he has been on the run for quite some time.

INTRODUCTION

On the other hand, everyone knows that there are ads that people talk about, that become water-cooler topics, that are so infectious that people voluntarily share them with others.

The average time it takes people to look at an ad is 1.7 seconds. This may come as a shock. But the time between Oliver Bierhoff's receiving the ball until the first Golden Goal in soccer history was only 1.7 seconds. Still, millions of people can remember it. And the time between Muhammad Ali's last punch during the "Rumble in the Jungle" until George Foreman's head hit the floor was also only 1.7 seconds. Almost forty years later, this moment has not been erased from the memory of millions.

Modern communication is not about turning 1.7 seconds into 2.7 seconds. It is about turning those 1.7 seconds into a lasting "A-ha!" event that will last through the next decision situation. The Hamlet question of advertising is no longer "To break through or to fall through?" Impact was so 20th century.

MOMENTUM
IS THE FORCE THAT COMMUNICATION NEEDS TODAY.

How can communication transform casual interest into lasting consciousness?

Psychologists call the smallest perceptible unit of time "momentum." For humans, it lasts about 1/18th of a second. Two stimuli succeeding each other in this interval are still perceived separately.

INTRODUCTION

In physics, momentum is the product of two physical entities—mass and speed—and means "directed thrust." Advertising has momentum when conviction and enthusiasm are concentrated in the same moment. When it creates a lasting experience in the blink of an eye.

Advertising with momentum is like a toy car with a flywheel. When it hits an obstacle, its true power becomes apparent. Advertisers always try to suggest security by using formulas for evaluating ads.

These formulas may be useful in evaluating the relevance of a campaign for target group, brand, or market. But they say nothing about a campaign's creative quality. No theory has been able to relax the tension between advertising's opposing missions—to entertain and to persuade.

Momentum precisely marks the interface between entertainment and persuasion. The moment when an advertising idea transforms attention into didactic success. High momentum not only addresses the senses but also gives a new direction to the way of thinking.

INTRODUCTION

THIS MEANS THAT IT DOESN'T JUST TURN HEADS
BUT ALSO TURNS SOMETHING INSIDE THE HEADS.

How does one recognize this cumulative power? Unfortunately, in many cases only after the fact. There is no foolproof recipe because the emotional aspect decides. In this we share the suffering of our colleagues in the entertainment industry. Everything starts there with a lot of wishing and hoping and everyone's hindsight is 20/20.

The only things you can calculate are the prerequisites for momentum — the message and the advertising idea. They must fuse into an inseparable nucleus. And unleash a targeted thrust that can be felt immediately. Not just after an advertising consultant has reeled off his sales pitch.

But only the rare truffle pigs in the advertising sector are able to sniff out the defining size, the intensity of the momentum. And only when they're lucky! Therefore, this book cannot give definitive answers. But it can inspire with examples and help cultivate gut feeling. Let's go!

P.S.:
We sprinkled our book with advertising work from Jung von Matt's first two decades. Kind of like commercial interruptions. These ads, posters, and TV spots are not always connected to the chapter they appear in — they simply illustrate our intention, and give practical examples of campaigns with proven momentum.

CHAPTER 1

THE LEVER PRINCIPLE OF COMMUNICATION
ABOUT THE ECONOMIC SIGNIFICANCE OF GREAT IDEAS

In Brussels, Europe's capital, two attractions vie for an audience: the Atomium, which is 102 meters tall, and Grand Place, which is 110 meters long.

The Atomium was completed after 18 months of construction for the 1958 World's Fair. It represents an iron crystal, with nine atoms magnified by 165 billion, and weighs 2,400 tons. Each atom is 18 meters in diameter.

The construction of Grand Place dragged on for centuries. Master builder Jacob van Tienen started building City Hall in 1402, but construction of the square continued into the 19th century.

The Atomium and Grand Place are among the costliest structures of their times. Both are fascinating and unique. But neither of them can win the duel, because the hands-down favorite is just a few blocks away. It is only 61 centimeters tall, and has become world-famous: Manneken Pis.

How can 61 centimeters attract more attention than 100 meters? How can something so small beat something so big? Only by a special force called "momentum."

THE LEVER PRINCIPLE OF COMMUNICATION

Grand Place is primarily beautiful. The Atomium is primarily tall. Neither quality is sufficient to trigger a thought process. But putting a fountain in a public place into which somebody is continually peeing—that's original and unprecedented. And it involves more than conventional giganticism.

If the stream of water came out of his mouth or ears nobody would notice the otherwise inconspicuous little man on that gray street corner.

The cute little pisser does more than just illustrate the power of an idea. He illustrates the concept of momentum in advertising. A spoiled intellect no longer reacts to conventional communication, it simply stores information without processing it. Déjà-vu. Everything stays the same. To reach the intellect, you must create a cognitive dissonance, trigger a thought process. Provoke a "Huh?!"

The fact that a series of myths revolve around Manneken Pis also shows that the statue has emotional power. Legend has it that a little man is supposed to have saved Brussels from a fire by peeing on it. Or that a little boy once peed against a witch's front door, and she became so angry that she transformed him into a statue.

It is also fitting that Manneken Pis is lovingly dressed up by his fellow citizens: as Dracula, as Elvis, as an ice hockey star, or as Santa Claus. All in all, he has accumulated about 800 costumes.

To create something that generates momentum in young and

old, all over the world, it takes more than size or beauty—it takes the allure of "That's impossible!"

THE MOST BEAUTIFUL WOMEN IN THE WORLD

can cause a sensation and—if they happen to appear on a poster wearing only their underwear—cause accidents. But it only becomes momentum if the ad surprises the viewer.

If a priest preaches in a diving suit it will probably trigger something. But only when he creates a surprising connection between his gospel and his outfit does he generate momentum. Only then does he spark a thought process in his astonished congregation.

Of course, momentum requires abandoning the usual communication patterns. And inevitably breaking new ground. Just like the priest uses remarkability to ensure memorability.

Electricity needs energy. It is only with an impulse, an exterior force, that we can generate momentum and break through the principle of energy conservation in déjà-vu.

Momentum begins beyond the usual, the secure, the ordinary.

A frequent point of conflict between client and ad agency is this. Both agree that they want to produce a piece of fascinating advertising. The problem is that the client wants his ad to

THE LEVER PRINCIPLE OF COMMUNICATION

show human strength. He wants to show good-looking people communicating with each other in peaceful harmony.

But the ad agency knows that fascination begins where the ideal world ends. Human foibles are what make a TV spot memorable. Because perfection is interchangeable and neither differentiates nor excites. Because perfection is, simply, boring. There are a million examples that illustrate this principle.

The Audi spot, in which the driver forgets where the tank is. The spot for the savings bank Sparkasse, in which the new-born baby thinks his daddy is stupid. The spot for the gasoline chain DEA, in which high-octane driver Super Ingo accidentally fills up with diesel.

THE WORLD SIMPLY LOVES LOSERS
MORE THAN WINNERS.

Just look at the most successful TV shows. Human weaknesses play a part everywhere. They even play the lead in the hit show "Big Brother." Corners and edges are exciting. Normality leaves you cold.

We will use an image from motor sports to explain this effect. There we have the so-called ideal line, which is the path that gets you around the course in the safest and fastest way. The ideal line has only one flaw: since everybody uses it, it becomes impossible to pass. If you want to pass, you have to switch to the fighting line, which is dirtier and riskier. But it is the only way to advance.

The same holds true for communication. Only if you stray from the ideal line can you pass your competitors. Only if you deviate from the ideal image, the ideal dramaturgy, the ideal font, the ideal people, can you rouse enthusiasm.

IT IS VITAL TO KNOW THE MOST IMPORTANT RULES OF COMMUNICATION.
IT MAKES IT EASIER TO BREAK THEM.

Because advertising ideas are in a pitched battle. And the harder everyone tries, the higher the bar gets raised. A nicely made, smart commercial spot can't generate momentum these days. The dosage needs to be higher. And adverse effects have not been reported.

Advertising might sometimes omit things but it can almost never go wrong. The risk is substantially lower than is frequently assumed. The consumer always sees ads in a positive light. He has learned that advertising is a form of communication that presents products or services positively. And that's how he understands it. And that's why we can assume his goodwill.

If, in an ad, the word "power" is written above the picture of a car, the consumer immediately recognizes that high, not low, power is meant. If "bitch" is written above a woman, he knows that it is not meant in a negative, but in an ironic way.

WELLA "FLAG," PRINT 2000:
HOW DO YOU TURN BEAUTIFUL HAIR INTO A BRAND PRODUCT? BY GIVING IT A TRADEMARK. TO IMPLEMENT THE WELLA CAMPAIGN IN 140 COUNTRIES WE FOUNDED WORLD FORCE, A MULTI-CULTURAL DEPARTMENT WITH THE TASK OF TRANSFERRING OUR CAMPAIGNS INTO OTHER CULTURAL AREAS WITHOUT LOSING EFFECTIVENESS.

PHOTOGRAPHER: JENS STUART

THE LEVER PRINCIPLE OF COMMUNICATION

You can get attention simply by using a picture that has never been seen before. But a simple stimulus is not sufficient to achieve momentum. To achieve momentum, you need a new thought, an impulse from outside. Not just a purely formal idea, but a conceptual idea.

When we were given the task of creating a new communication concept for Wella, the client complained about bad branding in existing ads. They tried to compensate for this weakness by using up to five trademark placements per ad.

We solved the problem with a new concept. Our thinking: we'll make beautiful hair into a trademark product. And we'll label it the way established world brands label their products. Discretely, on the face of the watch, like Rolex. Discretely, on the inner pocket, like Armani. Discretely, in the ear, like Steiff teddy bears. We placed a small Wella logo right in the hair.

The effect was overwhelming, even to us. The small logo didn't just beat the five large logos from the old ads, it also beat the large-format logo of our main competitor. The new concept couldn't be beaten with size. Small and smart beats big and stupid.

But momentum is not created only by how communication appears but also by where it appears.

THE STORY OF DAVID AND GOLIATH
ALSO TAKES PLACE IN COMMUNICATION.
EVERY DAY, AGAIN AND AGAIN.

THE LEVER PRINCIPLE OF COMMUNICATION

How did Jung know that they grow corn in Schleswig-Holstein? He read it while taking a winter walk. On a placard on the side of the road. He had never in his life been interested in corn-growing in Schleswig-Holstein.

If a trailer on TV had announced: "Now let's turn to corn-growing in Schleswig-Holstein," he would have immediately started zapping. He wouldn't have read a 10-line article in the tabloid Bild nor a longer commentary in the daily paper F.A.Z. Let alone a long corn-on-the-cob pictorial in the weekly magazine Stern.

He read the text for one reason only. Because he was starved for communication. Beggars can't be choosers—they will read an in-flight magazine, or even an old issue of Frau im Spiegel in the urologist's waiting room.

That placard was the first piece of communication Jung had encountered after a two-hour hike. He was glad that someone wanted to communicate something to him. (For the remainder of his walk he pondered the question of why he had read that sign, and, most of all, the question: "What can we learn from this about media planning?")

This first, basic principle holds true for all methods of advertising—the more bundled the messages, the more satiated the consumer, and the less effective the effect of each individual message.

BMW "TWO HEADLIGHTS," TV SPOT 2001:
HOW OFTEN ARE ADVERTISERS CONFRONTED WITH INTERCHANGEABLE PRODUCTS! IT'S REFRESHING WHEN WE GET THE CHANCE TO ADVERTISE A TRULY REVOLUTIONARY INNOVATION. BMW BUILT THE FIRST TWO-WHEEL VEHICLE WITH ALL THE SAFETY FEATURES OF A STANDARD SIZE CAR. THE SPOT RAN ALL OVER EUROPE AND WON THE GOLDEN LION AWARD IN CANNES.

DIRECTOR: PAUL ARDEN
PRODUCTION: ARDEN SUTHERLAND-DODD

THE LEVER PRINCIPLE OF COMMUNICATION

In communication, context is everything. A Scotsman muttering "hoots mon you've gottae bae taken the pusch!" stands out more in the Souks of Marrakech than at Harrod's in London, totally independent of whether it applies more to one place or the other. In the Souks, people will turn around when they hear something like that, at Harrod's they won't. Momentum, in the true sense of the word.

A BMW ad in a wine guide generates more momentum than in the magazine "auto motor und sport. " As does a Taittinger champagne ad in a car magazine. The prerequisite for straying from the beaten path is, of course, that you will still encounter your target audience.

The farmer's market theory that you sell the most where the rest of your competitors are does not apply to media planning. Its message must stand out in some way, it must surprise, be the only one on the left or right. Like the placard on the side of the road. Like the Scot in the Souks.

Or like some of the surprising media ideas we have been able to realize with our agency. Once we were checking out the Hamburg airport for unusual advertising possibilities. That's where we noticed that people are hardly ever more bored, or, in other words, more hungry for stimulation, than while they wait for their luggage. This is how the baggage claim carousel suitcases for the rental car company Sixt got their start. Then the newspaper-reading mannequins in the departure halls. Later, we also printed ads on the plastic tray that hold passengers' coats and valuables during safety checks.

Another media idea that was born in the airport was the pick-up people for the Sunday paper "Welt am Sonntag." On Sundays, we had students stand at the arrivals gate with signs that read: "Helmut Kohl." And in small print below: "is writing today in Welt am Sonntag."

We received worldwide attention for our commercial break event for BMW. We booked a whole commercial block on one of Germany's biggest private TV stations SAT.1 and let a BMW drive through all the commercials. This didn't just score the highest viewer ratings ever, but also garnered a lot of praise in trade papers. Including a full page article in the Financial Times.

We also generated great media response when we flooded the skyscraper office buildings of major banks in Frankfurt with huge projection spotlights to announce the initial public offering of shares for the online broker Consors. All through the night before the IPO the projections read: "Your fees are just as high" and

> "YOUR ARCHITECTS ARE MORE INVENTIVE THAN YOUR INVESTMENT ADVISORS."

Unfortunately, congeniality between creative agencies and media agencies in developing unusual advertising strategies is rare. The more the media business turns into mass business, the more media planners swim with the great (money) current and recommend time-tested placements.

THE LEVER PRINCIPLE OF COMMUNICATION

Despite the fact that a message becomes more memorable the farther away it is from other messages. Quantitatively and qualitatively. And since messages are crowding the favorite advertising media, only the latter seems at all useful: qualitative distance.

A plan for using alternative media that demonstrably doubles the desired effect would leave everybody puzzled. Something must be wrong here. Maybe circulation and range were getting mixed up? Or net range with gross range? Or British Pound with euro? But nobody is puzzled when a surprising media idea yields twice the effect.

Of course, it takes courage to stray from the beaten path, to deviate from the ideal line. To put an entire budget into one medium. Or to put spotlights on the Deutsche Bank.

Speaking of banks. Every enlightened person knows the irrefutable principle of investing—if you want higher returns, you must accept higher risk. If you are satisfied with moderate returns, you can minimize the risk.

Banks are obligated to bring this to their customers' attention and have them confirm their willingness to take risks. The customer chooses from a range of options between "low risk = low return" and "high risk = high return." The investor does this without complaint.

But why is it so difficult for advertising professionals to comprehend that advertising follows the same principle: the risk–return principle of communication?

ONLY IF YOU ARE WILLING TO TAKE RISKS CAN YOU EXPECT A BETTER THAN AVERAGE RETURN.

But if you always go for the sure thing from the start you can't expect any surprising effects. No positive ones either.

An ad agency's customer is usually not willing to take risks. He checks off "high security" but is not willing to settle for a lower return. But he is also not willing to take a higher risk.

What a pity! Because the return on a better idea can be huge. Let's take a look at Hollywood to illustrate this. A mediocre film might recoup production costs. But a successful film doesn't just gross 10% or 20% more. It gets a 1000% return, like "Independence Day," "Titanic," or the most successful German movie of all time, "Der Schuh des Manitu."

Or even 4,500%, like "The Blair Witch Project." That film cost less than US-$30,000 to produce and became a worldwide phenomenon. In front of the camera were a bunch of unknowns. Behind the camera were a bunch of unknowns. It couldn't have been cinematographic finesse. It was just a simple, surprising script, between fiction and reality, plus a clever pre-sale Internet strategy that catapulted the film to success.

Evidently, an unusual idea is the best way to mass market a product. This means that creativity is the economic factor with the greatest leverage.

THE LEVER PRINCIPLE OF COMMUNICATION

In 1983, Nicolas Hayek was sent to a watch factory as official receiver. Instead of liquidating the company he tried something unusual. He organized workshops with employees and young designers, and created a new, profitable business: Swatch.

The disruption of routines and expectations can achieve surprisingly successful results. Most importantly, it is necessary to interrupt the "more of the same."

Wherever parameters can be changed through creative ideas, momentum is possible. Wherever empirical knowledge is the only source for optimization, one has to make do with less.

For example, you can fiddle with a Formula One engine for a long time and have to be satisfied with a 5% increase in capacity. You can spend the same amount of time to fashion new investment strategies and have to be satisfied with a 5% increase in returns.

But an outstanding creative idea can move (percentage) mountains. All you need is the confidence that you have an idea with momentum. And the courage to present it.

Even people for whom a single mistake can have terrible consequences know that risk is a prerequisite for success. The title of a speech given by Reinhold Messner was:

SUCCESS. THE RISK OF FAILURE.

Courage has an effect on more than just the realization of an advertising idea; it can also influence the message. How easy is it for a politician to beat his opponent if he makes a concrete promise instead of repeating clichés? Or for a love-struck suitor to get a "yes" if he proposes to the object of his affections instead of merely waxing poetic about the sunset?

Jung often has breakfast in the same café as the guys from our cleaning company. Of course he greets them with a friendly nod, but he would never sit down at their table and ask them with great interest: "Are you motivated today?" Or give them instructions: "Please pay more attention to the receptionist's desk." Even if a dirty spot on the conference table irked him, he would never communicate it directly. And nobody would expect him to.

But here is the problem. Many company executives deal with their ad agency the way ad agency executive Jung deals with his cleaning company. As necessary service providers who do their job, whom you greet cordially when you happen to meet them, but whose problems you don't want to deal with and the details of whose efforts are of no particular interest. But not as providers of a more and more precious resource: communication.

A grievance in a time where communication can not only shape brands and sell products, but can also improve an entire company.

For example, by choosing an advertising message that makes a company perform to a particular standard. Unfortunately, this frightens many advertising departments:

DEUTSCHE BAHN "STEERING WHEEL," BILLBOARD 2000:
WE KEPT THIS IDEA ON HOLD FOR FIVE YEARS UNTIL A CHANGE IN THE BAHN'S MANAGEMENT MADE THEM READY TO TAKE THE RISK. OUR BAHN AD DIDN'T SET OUT TO VILIFY CARS. IT WAS ACTUALLY TRYING TO SHOW THE BAHN'S NEW SELF-CONFIDENCE AND SUPPORT ITS MORE THAN 300,000 EMPLOYEES.

PHOTOGRAPHER: KAI-UWE GUNDLACH

THE LEVER PRINCIPLE OF COMMUNICATION

"We can't make this promise because we can't keep it." And thus they fail to challenge and motivate the most important target group in the world—their own employees. A better, more productive attitude would be:

> "IF WE ARE GOING WITH THIS ADVERTISEMENT, WE MUST KEEP THIS PROMISE."

When we took over the Mövenpick account, the Swiss restaurant chain's image was ailing. And not without reason. The quality of service, marred by too many management changes, was a far cry from what founder Ueli Prager had created. From our point of view, the time was overdue for a campaign directed mainly inward, by obligating every single employee. We proposed this slogan to the Mövenpick people: "Mövenpick makes you happy."

We found out from a preliminary poll that the message was polarizing. Many of the respondents thought the promise was exaggerated, inappropriate, and, especially for Mövenpick, impossible to keep. Here's a typical response from a man in his forties: "A woman can make me happy perhaps, but a bowl of ice cream? I don't know." But a second observation assured us that this slogan would have momentum. "Mövenpick makes you happy" made everybody give a damn. It provoked and amused. Every respondent had an emotional reaction. It triggered interaction. It turned disgruntled pedestrians into engaged test subjects.

Mövenpick was perceptive enough to use the slogan, which was soon on everyone's lips. Only one recommendation was rejected. We had wanted every waiter and waitress to wear a button on his or her lapel that said: "I'm making you happy." But the marketing guys couldn't go that far. For the restaurant owner, "Mövenpick makes you happy" was clearly enough happiness.

In another case, von Matt couldn't push through an obligating advertising idea. He was working for Bosch service centers, which wanted to use their trademark reliable service to set themselves apart from the wild bunch of independent car repair shops. The following slogan emerged: "We don't do everything. But we do everything perfectly."

More than 900 independent Bosch partners were there for the presentation and greeted the slogan with enthusiasm. When the applause finally subsided, one audience member rose to respond. A master mechanic from Germany's Saarland region remarked softly that he was always striving for perfection, but that sometimes mistakes couldn't be avoided. He could not stand by that slogan in good faith.

His honest concern deflated the euphoria. Others raised their hands and agreed. And five minutes later the slogan was as dead as a corpse and the desired momentum sputtered and died with it. While understandable on a human level, the concerns raised by the man from Saarland are deplorable from a professional viewpoint. Even if the claim for perfection is utopian. If Bosch repair services had committed to that slogan in the mid-70s, they would have constantly improved. They would have forced themselves to get better and better.

THE LEVER PRINCIPLE OF COMMUNICATION

Of course, they would have had to deal with the unpleasant consequences foreseen by the master mechanic. Having to confront disappointed customers. Having to answer inconvenient letters. But these consequences are exactly what might increase the performance of a product or even a whole company, as well as trust in a brand.

A brand like Sixt certainly has more leeway than Mövenpick or Bosch, since it only appeals to a narrowly defined, open-minded target audience. But every brand has to consider this: only those who stretch their own boundaries, who drain their

"THAT'S IMPOSSIBLE" ACCOUNTS

and who are willing to risk that onlookers might shake their heads in disbelief can expect maximum effect. Don't forget, courage doesn't just make an ad more interesting; it makes the sender more interesting too. Because courage is a virtue that bespeaks decisiveness, vitality, and energy, which in turn makes many brand identities look attractive. The courage displayed by Germany's railway service, Die Bahn, when it attacked other systems of transportation increased its momentum. And generated plenty of self-confidence within its own ranks.

They had the courage to show a chewed-up steering wheel of a car in a traffic jam. The provoking effect of this image can be illustrated by a letter to the editor of auto motor und sport that ended with the outraged motorist's remark: "A mouthful of steering wheel still tastes better than the food in the dining car."

CHAPTER 2

A GOOD HORSE HAS A TIGHT JUMP. GOOD ADVERTISING DOESN'T
ABOUT THE SELF-FULFILLING POWER OF AMBITIOUS GOALS

When von Matt's mother sat in a Munich beer garden for the first time, she ordered a small beer. The waiter replied with a curt "Why don't you come back when you're thirsty." Edith von Matt was shocked. But her son always remembers the incident when a client comes to him and says "we want to defend our market share."

"Why don't you come back when you're ready to increase it."

Of course, communication strengthens opinions. But first and foremost it changes opinions and creates new perspectives.

Because communication only shows its full potential when it can set something in motion. Thus, a typical prerequisite for great communication is that a brand wants to reach for the stars and achieve a goal. The more ambitious the better.

"When you reach for the stars, you may not quite get one, but you won't come up with a handful of mud either," according to advertising agency founder Leo Burnett. All the successful campaigns from our agency's earliest years were based on ambitious goals. Take Sixt. Or Bild. Or Audi.

A GOOD HORSE HAS A TIGHT JUMP. GOOD ADVERTISING DOESN'T

In each case movement and change were imminent. And an uneasy team on the client's side ensured that the advertised product would march proudly ahead of the communication. Or at least keep up with it.

No market success brought us more praise than Audi's transition from an unemotional, specs-heavy men's brand to the favorite car of a trend-aware generation. But what little part did we play in this? We only made a few TV spots.

The real success had completely different roots. Audi had started a concerted offensive. It was the harmonic synergy of a new generation of products, led by the A4, and a new showroom world. Classic advertising was just the whipped cream on top. Nothing more. But nothing less either.

People always ask us why we gave up Audi for BMW. And eight years later BMW for Mercedes-Benz. Certainly, quite an unusual path in our line of business when a service provider peddles its competence and basically chooses its own clients. But each one of these partnerships helped both sides advance from a content perspective.

And for all the passion we feel today for the brand with the world's highest momentum—Mercedes-Benz—, we are glad that even our former contacts at the other manufacturers still welcome us at events like the International Motor Show (IAA).

An important prerequisite for high momentum is synchronization. Everything must interact. A communications offensive must be accompanied by a product offensive, a service offensive, a distribution offensive, otherwise it remains ineffective. Momentum can only be driven to a new level if the impulse comes from everyone involved.

PEOPLE OFTEN TRY TO CHANGE THE WORLD WITH COMMUNICATION ALONE.

A surefire dud. Disappointment for the client. Burned celluloid, burned paper, burned money. It's like a coach who explains his strategy to only one player.

Audi had a vision and vehemently turned all the screws at the same time. That created high momentum. A perfect example of an integrated offensive that went far beyond pure communication. The Audi people understood what every successful soccer coach knows—that you have to attack to win the game. Playing four-player defensive line "catenaccio" is bound to fail.

The heart of our Audi campaign consisted of five TV spots. Even if none of them reached the huge momentum of the "Fan" TV spot with the bobbing Elvis, courtesy of our successors Saatchi & Saatchi, they were well known and popular. From the A6 TDI spot, where a man ponders the question "Where is the tank?" to the A8 "Aluminum" spot, in which eminent stock market guru André Kostolany warns "Stay away from steel stocks!"

But along with these five strong spots we produced five pretty weak ones, which luckily nobody remembers. The secret, they ran only briefly or not at all. The Audi marketing team cultivated something that could be called

PROMOTION OF THE BEST.

Equipped with the conviction that the true momentum of a TV spot doesn't show until it is completely shot and edited, they didn't decide whether to use an ad until the very end. Which meant scheduling a proven spot rather than a new, sub-par spot more in tune with the brand offensive.

How much more difficult it is to create advertising for a brand in a holding pattern! For a client who wants to conserve his image, who acts equally conservatively in his advertising! Projects of this nature are what we call preservation of historic monuments. An ambitious ad agency undoubtedly feels more challenged when it can create a new monument.

For clients who consider a defensive strategy the right thing for them, the favorite phrase is position of superiority. "We have to communicate from a position of superiority." Anything with a hint of confrontation is frowned upon. Just don't offend anyone. Every aggressive communication attempt is dismissed with "We don't need to do that sort of thing."

But a position of superiority is not only not a challenge for creative minds, it has increasingly become a real danger — the

A GOOD HORSE HAS A TIGHT JUMP. GOOD ADVERTISING DOESN'T

pride of communication that goes before a fall. Those who are silent today will die. Market leaders can no longer quietly defend their position. Communication follows the principle that attack is the best defense. Being in a position of superiority can easily become a slow poison.

When Sixt became Germany's number one rental car company, they were considering a change in strategy. After years of momentous offensive strategies, we pondered whether a campaign from a position of superiority would be better. Along the lines of "You don't become Germany's number one car rental company without good reason." But Mr. Sixt's instinct said no, the Sixt brand would lose its aggressive character and charm. And that's just what the business traveler values in the brand. So, Sixt remained on the offensive in their communications, even though there was nothing left to attack. And they have never relinquished their position to a competitor.

Of course, defensive work is also part of successful business. A company that has only a strong offense will suffer defeat in the long run, like the "Eleven Foals" of German soccer club Borussia Mönchengladbach in the 1970s, with their relentless offensive play. Those who only generate interest and gain customers won't be able to sustain their success. Still, advertising is not—even if it keeps getting wrongfully burdened with this task—a customer base retention tool; it is rather a customer base extension tool.

The most important factors for an effective defense of your customer base and market shares are product and service.

AUDI "WHERE IS THE TANK?," TV SPOT 1995:
ONE OF THE MOST FREQUENTLY QUOTED SPOTS OF THE AUDI CAMPAIGN. A LION AWARD WINNER IN CANNES. AND THE AGENCY'S FIRST SPOT THAT RAN IN 16 COUNTRIES. BUT IT HAD TO OVERCOME QUITE A FEW OBSTACLES BEFORE IT WAS PRODUCED. IS ADVERTISING ALLOWED TO MAKE A MAN DRIVING AN AUDI LOOK LIKE A FOOL? IF SO, IS IT ALLOWED TO MAKE A WOMAN LOOK LIKE AN EVEN BIGGER FOOL?

DIRECTOR: TARSEM
PRODUCTION: SPOTS FILMS

A GOOD HORSE HAS A TIGHT JUMP. GOOD ADVERTISING DOESN'T

Of all communication disciplines it is direct advertising that can make the most important contribution to a defensive strategy — that is, to customer retention. The Internet is also not on the offensive front line, perhaps in the second tier or further back. At the front line in the goal of conquering new customers is classic advertising.

That's why the typical client mantra "Winning new customers without offending the established ones" doesn't make much sense. It is nearly impossible to offend established users with advertising. A bad product might very well do that. Or sloppy service. Or a total lack of reasonable customer retention measures.

The above-mentioned mantra is not only useless, it is also frequently the culprit in bad advertising. Let's look at another soccer example. If you make your leading scorer play defense, you not only get a weaker defensive line but you also undermine his greatest strength: scoring goals. Just like you undermine advertising's greatest strength if you define customer retention as the primary goal, and make customer base acceptance the standard. A classic lose-lose situation.

Ever since we started creating ads for the German railway system, the Bahn, we have suffered from the frequent attacks against them as well. Evidently, the Bahn is considered a kind of people's property — even before the scheduled stock market IPO — that can be criticized by everyone.

There's the punctuality issue, for instance. For many years, the Bahn has been the most punctual transportation system by far.

A GOOD HORSE HAS A TIGHT JUMP. GOOD ADVERTISING DOESN'T

In most cases, you can set your watch by the Bahn's arrival times — something unimaginable for planes and automobiles. There is just one problem. Nobody wants to believe it.

If the Bahn is even a tiny bit late, considerable outrage ensues. Whereas a plane's half-hour delay is quickly forgiven. It's the air space's fault. Or the necessary safety checks. And cars are almost universally forgiven, particularly one's own: "This traffic jam is not my car's fault! The other cars are to blame."

We proposed to adjust this false perspective with a TV spot. Our compliments to the Bahn's new communications management team who mustered up the courage for this unusual offensive. The spot shows a 3-minute Bahn delay causing a minor riot. The gist: the best ones have the strictest judges. In 2001, the Bahn was still Germany's most punctual system of transportation.

Unfortunately, the spot ran at a time when construction was causing more delays than usual. This resulted in the spot getting by far the best attention-getting marks of all Bahn spots, but not in generating positive momentum. The many passengers who didn't have a negative experience with Bahn punctuality were enthusiastic. But others who had bad luck with delays were outraged. For these people, the TV spot enhanced a negative image.

Even as a young copywriter, von Matt loved ambitious communications goals. At the end of the 1970s, Volvo was one of his customers, and with them he committed the only big blunder of his advertising career.

A GOOD HORSE HAS A TIGHT JUMP. GOOD ADVERTISING DOESN'T

He presented a radio campaign that was supposed to work like this. "In interviews, we'll collect testimonials to Volvo's positive image, compact it into statements that sharpen the brand's profile, and trumpet the results to the market." The customer was excited. High momentum ahead.

Now, the challenge was to get the testimonials. Von Matt and a sound engineer drove to the Irschenberg rest stop in Bavaria, where a lot of vacationers passed through, which meant that plenty of different dialects could be included in the campaign. His standard question was: "What to you associate with the brand 'Volvo'?" But the answers were disappointing: Swedish tank, massive, bad design. He was getting nothing that could be used in the ambitious radio spots.

Faced with this dilemma, von Matt used an underhanded trick. His new question was: "What do you associate with the brand 'Mercedes'?" And right away the answers he needed came pouring in: quality, longevity, safety, etc. Excellent Volvo spots went on the air. Until now, nobody knew about this deception. Luckily, it was

THE ONLY LIE
VON MATT HAS TO CONFESS TO IN MORE THAN FORTY YEARS OF ADVERTISING.

Ten years later, while working for Springer & Jacoby, von Matt had the chance to make real Mercedes advertising. At the first meeting with the brand executives it didn't seem like they were very aggressive. At the briefing, one of the board directors said, "And always remember: the Mercedes star is made of gold, all we did was chrome-plate it."

Nevertheless, the content of the resulting campaign, with the slogan "Fighter in Flannel," had some bite, even if it appeared understated and gray. A communications concept that has not lost any of its forward thrust over the course of a decade, and that ushered the brand into a new era.

The first TV spot shot for Mercedes was based, like many others, on personal experience. Von Matt had flown to Jerez a short while before to present a new campaign to the Jerez brandy makers. The trip was long and exhausting. The flight was terrible. And everything went wrong at the destination airport. But the rental car he got made up for everything: a brand-new Mercedes 190 E. Von Matt got into the car, closed the door, and was thinking to himself "Welcome home!" And he wrote down this story afterwards.

The TV spot achieved high momentum, but was booed in Cannes because of chauvinism. Sometimes the Swiss are more German than Germans. But this spot was the beginning of a great, long-term campaign for Springer & Jacoby, followed by a series of real gems. Because Mercedes did not hide behind the established propriety of the brand, but reached for the stars with both feet planted firmly on the ground.

The breakthrough for BMW as a high-end brand in the 1970s has a lot to do with aggressive tactics as well. Model policy,

BANK AUSTRIA/CREDITANSTALT "CHILD," TV SPOT, 2003:
IT IS UNUSUAL THAT ONE OF THE LARGEST
ADVERTISERS IN A COUNTRY IS ALSO ONE
OF THE MOST COURAGEOUS. OUR FIRST

communication, everything was designed to attack. And an upwardly mobile clientele showed their gratitude with enthusiasm.

Who knows if BMW had as much product substance then as it has today? Perhaps not, since there was that unforgettable heckler during a general meeting, "When will your products be as good as your advertising?" But the brand's unstoppable rise began with the joy of communication, the joy of conquering new market segments, and of course the joy of one's own success.

An ad from that period, which was never published, was a subtle attack on the Mercedes star that BMW's ad agency at the time used to introduce BMW's superior engine quality. The headline read:

"OUR STATUS SYMBOL IS UNDER THE HOOD."

Americans have used this special type of aggressive, confrontational tone for decades in their comparative advertisements. They don't hesitate to run a tank over a European car to prove that the advertised American equivalent is tougher.

For a few years, comparative advertising has been allowed in Germany as well — with certain restrictions and conditions, but allowed nevertheless. Comparative advertising has opened a number of new possibilities. At last, it is possible to show the competition's limits. And consumers could be the big winners because comparison leads to transparency. But the first big winners turned out to be the lawyers.

Comparative advertising is difficult in practice. It requires comparison based solely on understandable facts. Anything that degrades the competitor is still prohibited. It's like a karate championship: all hits can only be fake; a real hit will be disqualified immediately. And a really hard hit can be sued for damages.

Besides, comparative advertising does not necessarily yield high momentum. Neither in terms of ethics and taste nor in terms of efficiency. Shouting out the competition's flaws like a fishmonger doesn't retain customers. Just as the consumer is attracted by fair competition, impertinent mud slinging irritates him.

NO WOMAN CAN BE WON
BY BADMOUTHING HER EX.

On the contrary. Badmouthing is unappealing.

Forceful persuasion stems from one's own capabilities. Parallel comparisons that stress one's own capabilities simply have to be charming and be delivered with a wink. They have to demonstrate — and the phrase applies in this context — their position of superiority.

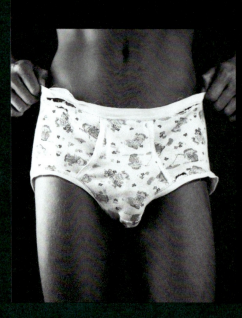

ViELe MäNNeR veRhütEN, oHNe eS zu woLLeN.

Nicht nur beim Flirten gut: Alte Maschen ziehen heute nicht mehr. Deshalb nehmen wir für unsere Slips nur hochwertige, moderne Stoffe und uns für die Verarbeitung mehr Zeit. Das Ergebnis: schöne, gut sitzende Slips, die beim zarten Geschlecht garantiert ankommen.

MEY FINE BODYWEAR "BIRTH CONTROL," PRINT 2000:
HEADLINE: "A LOT OF MEN USE BIRTH CONTROL AND DON'T EVEN KNOW IT."
THERE IS NO UNDERWEAR MANUFACTURER WHO INVESTS MORE QUALITY AND LOVE FOR DETAIL IN HIS PRODUCTS THAN MEY. IT IS UP TO THE PRINT CAMPAIGN TO MAKE THE PRESENTATION AS INTERESTING AND VARIED AS POSSIBLE, IN THIS CASE WITH OVER 130 IMAGES SINCE 1995.

PHOTOGRAPHER: UWE DÜTTMANN

A GOOD HORSE HAS A TIGHT JUMP. GOOD ADVERTISING DOESN'T

The historic advertising example for successful aggressiveness is the case of Avis in the 1960s. DDB, the trend-setting agency at that time, accepted the relatively unimportant car rental company as a customer only with the assurance of complete creative control. Avis executive Robert Townsend agreed to the unusual bargain.

A legendary campaign ensued: "We are only No. 2. But we try harder." To this day, it remains a model for ad copywriters. With each ad, Avis was challenging market leader Hertz, presenting the competitor as big and competent, but also bloated and spoiled. And Avis was the hungry up-and-comer.

Hertz took up the gauntlet and parried, resulting in a duel that actually yielded three victors. Hertz, who could enhance their position as market leader. Avis, who was far from being number two at the outset of the campaign, but became the runner-up in the end. And America's business travelers, who avidly followed the advertising duel, siding with either Avis or Hertz as if they were religions.

Of course there were also losers: all the car rental companies that were not part of the duel, and who went unnoticed.

If a client has the guts and his market position allows for such an approach, competitive advertising can set a lot of things in motion and heighten everyone's involvement. Because it is pure competition and offers a detailed picture of the enemy: "This is our opponent. We must be better, faster and, most of all, different than him."

A GOOD HORSE HAS A TIGHT JUMP. GOOD ADVERTISING DOESN'T

In 1994, an underwear manufacturer from the southern German region of Swabia was fed up with losing business to global designer labels and started an offensive. That yielded a campaign that was a bit too big for their britches, but added a few sizes to the brand "Mey fine Bodywear."

Northern Germans would probably think that the Mey family enterprise is rather stingy, a typical trait for most Swabians. For example, when Marcus Schenkenberg, the most beautiful man in the world, asked to keep the three Mey briefs he had worn for the ad photo shoots, the answer came promptly: "Our pleasure! And where may we send the bill?"

The company displays its generous side only if it will result in visibility for the brand. Buying precious Pima cotton from the Piura region in northern Peru. During manufacturing and quality assurance. But for their advertising as well. They never doubted a double-page ad, an unusual format for an underwear brand.

A special example of Mey's generosity was the way they provided additional motivation for the ad agency. Every new idea received a democratic vote, with equal weight given to ad agency reps present at the meeting. Let's dare a hypothesis:

> IF ALL COMPANIES
> WERE JUST A LITTLE BIT LIKE MEY
> THERE WOULD NEVER BE ANOTHER ECONOMIC CRISIS.

Since we have taken over their account, the company has only once cut the wrong corners. When a customer complained via

A GOOD HORSE HAS A TIGHT JUMP. GOOD ADVERTISING DOESN'T

e-mail about the change from the German slogan "Mey feine Wäsche" to the English "Mey fine Bodywear," she immediately received an e-mail response. It read: "Then why don't you buy your underpants somewhere else, bitch!"

True to the company's philosophy of investing only if it furthered the brand, they had neglected to install a network security system, and a malicious hacker was able to get into their electronic network.

Another of our clients showed their aggressive side in a spectacular event. The Milchstrasse publishing group sponsored the jerseys for the prominent soccer team Hamburger Sport-Verein (HSV), and they had to watch helplessly as an absolutely miserable season came to an end. With the logo of their magazine TV Spielfilm on each player's chest.

Suffering considerably, the publisher intended to reduce the HSV players' remuneration. But CEO Martin Fischer had a better idea. He suggested "Let's forbid the club to wear our logo for the last few games." One phone call and the team had to play the next game with an ad-free chest—virtually naked.

It was the best advertising idea for TV Spielfilm in the last decade, and it didn't come from us. The evening news reported it. All the newspapers reported it. Never before had jersey advertising been this eye-catching. The HSV lost the remaining games of the season as well. And the name of the winner: TV Spielfilm.

CHAPTER 3

IF YOU HAVE SOME-THING IMPORTANT TO SAY, DON'T USE LONG SENTENCES
ABOUT CONCENTRATION AND REDUCTION

When Jung was at a Roxy Music concert many years ago, he was pretty amazed. For starters, every person present could be counted among the trendy crowd. Appropriately styled of course, since everything surrounding Bryan Ferry was a fashion event as well.

But that was not all that amazed him. In the middle of a pack of the most ardent fans, there was a girl trying her utmost to get the charismatic singer's attention. First of all, she showed a lot of herself. But other girls around her did too. That's why she thought of something else to bring her high momentum. A cardboard sign with five letters.

You know these attempts to express passion. Usually, the sign says "I love you!" Or the name of the adored star, so he recogvnizes that the message is directed at him, not at the greasy-haired drummer behind him. But in light of the strong competition the girl must have thought, I only have one choice—provoke or lose.

IF YOU HAVE SOMETHING IMPORTANT TO SAY, DON'T USE LONG SENTENCES

Her sign said:

"I'M WET."

It is likely that Bryan Ferry still remembers those words, more indicative of her attitude than her physiological condition. They also bespoke her assertive originality.

And that's what communications experts like us get paid for—broad, poster-like extracts that don't just represent facts but trigger a process. And ignite momentum. Words, sentences, quotes that open up a whole world. Messages that don't get stuck in your head but make it all the way down to your gut.

Human memory can be described as a data processor that we use to store information—stories, for example—and retrieve it when necessary. It is often compared to a computer, but while certain important features are similar, remembering is far more than just retrieving information.

An important part of remembering something is the conviction that certain stories or episodes we remember have something to do with us, are connected to other events, experiences, or desires. But our daily life is also influenced by actions that we are able to perform without having to remember the specific conditions of the learning process. For instance, when we use our language, perform a routine work sequence, or go skiing. We can do all these things, but there is no subjective experience of remembering every time we do.

Cognitive scientists differentiate between the semantic memory, which stores conceptual and factual knowledge, and the procedural memory, which we use to learn skills and acquire habits. It is important to be aware of this difference because we can only remember something if the information to be retrieved can be connected to a specific time and place.

At some point we came up with

THE SMALL PODIUM THEORY.

It describes a consumer tendency often present in market research, that you only remember the three best TV spots in a commercial block, only the three best ads in a magazine, and only the three best posters during a car ride. The three athletes who get to climb the podium at the Olympics are the only ones we remember. Number four already belongs to the tragic Club of the Forgotten. Also ran...

A dark example of this theory was September 11, 2001. If someone had told you about a mad plan to crash a passenger plane into the Pentagon, you could be sure it would have been the lead story in the international press.

But it didn't happen like that. Hardly anyone talked about the devastating act of terror at the Pentagon, none of those pictures made it to the front page. Simply because the attacks on the World Trade Center and the crash in Pittsburgh were even more dramatic events that happened on the same day.

JUNG v MATT/Neckar

MERCEDES-BENZ "SORRY," TV SPOT 2010:
THE INVENTOR OF THE AUTOMOBILE HAS BEEN THE DRIVING FORCE FOR INNOVATION TO THIS DAY. IT WAS THE GOAL OF A TV SPOT, CREATED FROM OUR OWN INITIATIVE, TO STRENGTHEN THIS FACT. THANKS TO THE OPENNESS AND FLEXIBILITY OF MERCEDES-BENZ'S MARKETING TEAM, WE WERE ABLE TO SHOW THE SPOT IN A NUMBER OF MARKETS.

DIRECTOR: ALEX FEIL
FILM PRODUCTION: ELEMENT E FILMPRODUKTION GMBH

IF YOU HAVE SOMETHING IMPORTANT TO SAY, DON'T USE LONG SENTENCES

Back to the perfect world of advertising. We have to concentrate all our talent to make sure we are one of those three most fascinating, outstanding, original, provoking, and attractive advertising ideas in our immediate surroundings.

But our duty for concentration goes beyond that. Even in first, second, or third place we hold a ticket for only a little bit of attention that will soon become invalid. We have not landed with the consumer—we have only found the approach. For an actual landing, our message must concentrate on the essentials.

Some advertisers think the consumer sits in front of the TV as if he were a contestant on "Am laufenden Band," an old game show in which the ambitious candidates watched a moving conveyor belt and, in 30 seconds, had to recall as many of the prizes that had just passed by them as they could. An expensive mistake.

The consumer sits there like this. Bored—there are no prizes to win, after all. A little annoyed—the show he was watching got interrupted. Distanced—like anyone who is asked to consider something he never asked for in the first place.

THE CONSUMER MAGNANIMOUSLY ALLOWS US TO DELIVER OUR MESSAGE.

But only one, please. And only if we present it in a very, very charming way. As we mentioned before, the maxim of "Demand a lot and you will get a lot" fails in communication. Momentum is reserved for those who are modest.

There is the legendary image with the tennis balls. If one ball is thrown at you, you will catch it. If five are thrown at you, you will catch none. We developed our own image that has something to do with communication and that you come across more frequently in everyday life than tennis balls.

Imagine you are sitting in a conference room and a man enters. "My name is Woodhouse." There is a good chance that you will remember his name. And if the man turns out to be important for you during the meeting you will likely be able to recall his name later. Now, you are sitting in a conference room and a group of people enters. "Woodhouse, Granger, Buck, Ross, Williams, Stewart, Miller." You won't remember a single one, not even Mr. Woodhouse.

Because there are so many of them, you won't even make an effort to remember one of the names. And if a person turns out to be important for you during the meeting, it is too late anyway, since you didn't remember the name in the beginning.

That's why business cards were invented. And that's why the successful advertiser focuses on only one message per medium. Because exactly the same thing happens with marketing communication. If you limit yourself to one new message, you stand a good chance of being remembered.

IF YOU HAVE SOMETHING IMPORTANT TO SAY, DON'T USE LONG SENTENCES

THOSE WHO AMBUSH THE CONSUMER WITH A BUNCH OF MESSAGES WILL ONLY DELIVER THE BUNCH, NOT THE MESSAGE.

Compare if you will the momentum of "He brought me a rose" and "He brought me a bouquet of spring flowers." And compare the cost–benefit ratio! One flower can have more power than a bouquet. Even if the bouquet seems more impressive.

Advertising only has momentum when the consumer learns the message and transforms it into a lasting memory. How does this happen? Psychologists have an easy answer. It is easiest for us to learn and retain information if it is imbedded in a story and visualized with images. These will evoke certain familiar emotions. Psychologists call it coding.

Images should be connected by a chronologically structured story that corresponds to our thought processes. Stories do the coding for us. They help us to remember information at a later point.

Memory artists also use this technique when they manage to recall impossibly long number sequences. Their trick is that every number is tied to an event in a story.

There is hardly a difference between stories that are personally experienced and those that are recounted. Even recounted stories become an experience as they are told, since they have a direct connection with experienced stories. Otherwise we would not understand them.

In an era with very different co-existing lifestyles, it is important to take into account the audience's shared experiences when telling a story. "Great" stories that have formed the identity, culture, or tradition of a society up to this point are replaced by smaller stories like those offered by advertising.

They pick up and continue stories we may have heard or experienced elsewhere—probably in a very different context. In advertising, however, this is not that simple, for at least three reasons. First, the stories must be connected to the message in such a way that they are understandable and easy to follow. Second, the stories also have to fulfill their task as communication. And third, there is only a limited amount of time and space available for storytelling (the 20 seconds of an average TV spot or the 40 square centimeters of an average print ad, for example).

Luckily, headlines can help us out. A story is always tagged in our heads with a heading, a key word, or a name. In advertising, the tag is an unseen key image or a surprising headline.

We connect vacation experiences with where the events took place. "Do you remember our dinner on the beach in Bermuda?" Childhood experiences are just like that. When von Matt was little he hated red cabbage. It was served again and again and he kept refusing it. One day, his mother employed a ruse. She took the pot of red cabbage and asked

"WOULD ANYONE LIKE SOME MORE STRONG-MAKER?"

IF YOU HAVE SOMETHING IMPORTANT TO SAY, DON'T USE LONG SENTENCES

Von Matt was perplexed. His mother casually added: "Red cabbage is also called strong-maker because it makes you very strong." Immediately, red cabbage became his favorite food. The creative idea to simply call red cabbage "strong-maker" brought high momentum. This trick changed von Matt's attitude towards red cabbage. 50 years later, Japanese mothers give their kids "Gogaku Soba," the "Pass-your-exam noodles."

Over 60% of people involved with advertising cite creativity as the top criterion for choosing an ad agency. Creativity has become the key incentive for an entire sector. There are top creative teams, creative awards, creative milieus, the creative scene. And everybody swears by the added value of creative advertising and keeps trying to prove it empirically.

The rule of thumb is quite simple at first glance. The more creative the advertising, the more momentum it will generate, and the more immune it is against information overload and interchangeable products. There seems to be great unity among communications experts. It's the same kind of unity among physicians who think people should lead healthier lives. But what are the concrete measures?

What makes people healthier? Activity or rest? Enjoyment or abstinence? Traditional or homeopathic medicine? What exactly makes advertising more efficient? What kind of creativity leads to measurable success? The actual manifestations of creativity are probably as varied as people's opinions about creativity.

But just like one medication doesn't cure all ailments and must be used in the right dosage, creativity has to be administered with care. If applied correctly, it can perform miracles. The basic rule is, if the message is strong and the facts are compelling, you can go easy on the razzle-dazzle.

Of course, even the most interesting facts trigger an emotional effect only if they are presented appropriately. Without Dolly, the cloned sheep, genetic manipulation would not have become a topic of general debate as quickly as it did. An advertising message also has a longer lasting effect if it is emotionalized by an illustrative example. To demonstrate how smoothly a BMW runs, we stood a large coin on its edge on an engine block—and it became the most often read car ad of the year in Spiegel magazine.

But the use of creativity reaches its limits where momentum changes from a force that turns attention towards the product to one that turns attention away—where momentum overshoots its target.

For instance, we have had almost uniformly bad experiences with original ideas for job postings. This form of communication works differently than others. Contrary to the typical ad reader, who needs to be captured, the job seeker does not need any additional stimulus to deal with the offer. Unlike the casual reader of advertising, he comes already armed with high motivation.

Any type of creative enhancement would be more irritating than helpful for this person. And, by the way, the job search

BMW "TRANSPORTER," PRINT 2002:
HEADLINE: "A MERCEDES CAN BE FUN TO DRIVE, TOO."
AFTER MERCEDES LAUNCHED SEVERAL HARSH AD ATTACKS
AGAINST BMW, IT WAS TIME FOR THE JOY-OF-DRIVING IMPERIUM
TO FIGHT BACK. BUT WITH MORE ELEGANCE! COMPETITIVE
ADVERTISING CAN GENERATE HIGH MOMENTUM, IF IT MANAGES
TO PRESENT A BELIEVABLE PRODUCT ADVANTAGE WITH A WINK.

PHOTOGRAPHER: UWE DÜTTMANN

IF YOU HAVE SOMETHING IMPORTANT TO SAY, DON'T USE LONG SENTENCES

deals with the most important topic between life and death: the future.

Another example is the sales folder. It has to be clear and crisp. It has to present facts unsentimentally and to the point. Every irony, every exaggeration, every abstraction weakens it. That is why we are convinced that the best sales folder writer is not a copywriter but a salesman.

We also believe in certain kinds of creativity when it comes to social causes. While it might be possible to expose a grievance with drastic statements and images for a lasting effect, social issues and advertising cleverness rarely make good partners. "Original" is not the right tonality for a brand or an organization involved in social causes. It is hard to accept someone known to be smart or witty as a spokesperson for a cause that helps starving children.

The reason why there are so many creative social campaigns cannot be attributed to the fact that advertisers all have such big hearts. Ad agencies are desperately looking for jobs where nobody can argue with them, because they're doing it for heavenly rewards alone.

A creative idea helps when messages are interchangeable or where small differences need to be dramatized that would otherwise bore the consumer. Or those he would otherwise avoid.

Until the mid-70s, company strategies tried to adjust the company and its products to current market trends. Since then, companies have been trying to mold consumer desire to the product through active, target-oriented communication.

Simply because product life expectancies have shrunk as rapidly as development costs have grown. In addition to a variety of changes in modern society. Different lifestyles and orientation patterns seem to coexist without a problem. In this sense, companies are successful that manage to charge their products with emotional experience-based qualities in addition to mere functional use value.

Products symbolize lifestyles and offer orientation patterns. Communicating such marginal information is only possible when it is embedded in stories. That's what creativity is.

When additional incentives for retirement savings accounts— the so-called "Riester-Rente"— were introduced in 2001, many Germans were faced with the almost insurmountable problem of finding the right product in light of the variety of offers. The matter was too complex and insurance agents were too eager to make a deal. The government solved the problem by allowing only those products that had been certified to be sold. This created trust with the consumers. Trust is not a rational calculation but an emotional experience. Most of all, it helps us make decisions.

The consumer only lets something into his head that he accepts emotionally. And not the other way round. One of our credos is,

IDEAS MUST WORK IN THE GUT.

DEUTSCHE POST "ICE-CREAM IN THE MAIL," PRINT 2001:
A FINE EXAMPLE FOR SYMBOLIC EXAGGERATION THAT WAS UNDERSTOOD AND ACCEPTED BY THE AUDIENCE. COMMUNICATION IS LESS ABOUT REALITY THAN SENSUALITY: NO ONE BELIEVES THAT AN ICE-CREAM BAR CAN SIMPLY BE MAILED JUST LIKE THAT. BUT EVERYONE CAN SEE THAT THE POST OFFICE DELIVERS PARCELS EVEN FASTER NOW.

PHOTOGRAPHER: STEPHAN FÖRSTERLING

Not necessarily in the head. Something that is met with rational resistance can only be sold with emotions.

Every year the top executive of a large film production company invites von Matt to dinner. Von Matt is pleased to obliged, since the meetings are entertaining and the restaurants expensive, at the least. But the dinners have never led to a job because the decision for who gets to produce our films is not made in the head of our agency but in its guts, by the Creative Director.

Every successful salesman knows that a compliment to the secretary of the head of purchasing is more effective than the usual three bottles of wine for members of the finance committee at Christmas.

Why does advertising so often disregard this principle and enter the game at too high a level? It appeals to the head, to the human command center, rather than to the so-called lesser instincts where decisions for most purchases are made?

ADVERTISING OFTEN CONVINCES ON THE WRONG LEVEL.

The scientific proof is this. More than 90% of the time, the consumer shows only a limited willingness to deal with a topic. He only has "low involvement" and will only process the stimulus peripherally. He gives advertising a small amount of attention, and the processing will be cursory.

IF YOU HAVE SOMETHING IMPORTANT TO SAY, DON'T USE LONG SENTENCES

The way a highly involved consumer processes stimuli is pivotal—intense and with undivided attention. This situation is typical for a "plan buyer" who, unfortunately, only accounts for 1–10% of consumers.

The biggest challenge for marketing communication lies in transforming low involvement into high involvement. In other words, a shift from peripheral to central processing of stimuli (Lachmann, 2002). We can set up a simple rule:

The less involved the consumer is, the more surprising the effect of a thrilling story has to be.

Creating advertising for the Bahn (German railways) is challenging in that the audience is by no means highly involved, and the communication target is highly competitive. Because putting more traffic on the tracks means less traffic on the streets and in the air. We basically had to make a transportation system palatable for enthusiastic drivers or vacation jetsetters who had very little interest in it.

Anyone trying to prove to one of those drivers that it makes sense to leave their beloved cars at home has his work cut out for him. The more you argue with facts, the harder it gets. The heart of the matter is:
> YOU DON'T HAVE TO BELIEVE ADVERTISING,
> YOU HAVE TO WANT TO BELIEVE IT.

No German will stand to have his beloved car besmirched. If you start telling him about breakdowns, traffic jams, and gas prices, he'll be your fiercest enemy. And you don't buy

IF YOU HAVE SOMETHING IMPORTANT TO SAY, DON'T USE LONG SENTENCES

anything from your enemy. Creative communication can work wonders here. Because those who are charming and witty will be forgiven unpleasant facts. The court jesters of the Middle Ages could attest to that.

If our Bahn campaign had vilified the car, it couldn't have produced any significant momentum. But since it did it with a wink and a smile, it quickly became a success with the audience.

The competitive message was forgiven because it was presented with charm. During the 2000 World's Fair Expo we ran a series of TV spots in which several drivers asked pedestrians for directions. "Excuse me, what's the fastest way to get to Hannover?" After pondering briefly, the response was, "By train!" This campaign became the opening for the Bahn's new self-image.

What if the Bahn had demanded "Take the train or else you'll sit in traffic!" without the little exaggeration and the wink. Drivers would have flipped Bahn the bird.

We made that mistake once. We produced a TV spot in which the car was the harbinger of the apocalypse, the most evil, antiquated mode of transportation available. We showed scenes of "man versus car." At the peak of this demonization a few kids, still in shock, brought home a dead cat. This spot was a turn-off. It was very rational and too serious in tone. Despite its unusual length it got unsatisfactory ratings, which made marketing executive Gabriele Handel-Jung take it off the air quickly.

One of the main reasons why the bulk of advertising—not just in Germany, by the way—is uninspired is that discussions and decisions about advertising are very rational. In a rational meeting situation that is far removed from the emotional situation of a typical family evening in front of the TV.

Once, after one of those exhausting presentations in an air-conditioned conference room in a skyscraper, Jung came up with an idea for a presentation room—a cozy living room right in the middle of our agency, where TV commercials are presented. Based on the thesis that the most important decisions about advertising are made in a completely wrong environment. In an environment that disregards the warm hearth atmosphere of a typical TV evening.

Ambitious stereo salesmen often furnish their stores like a living room. The customer will feel more at home and get a more authentic impression of the equipment and the sound.

Even more ambitious stereo salesmen will carry the objects of desire into the customer's apartment for a risk-free listening test under real conditions. That was what Jung had in mind.

But in practice the problem often solves itself. Often, the executive will take a presentation home and make his decision in the presence of his loved ones. We're no different, by the way.

If a TV spot is presented in the rational atmosphere of a typical meeting situation, the aura quickly turns into a perishable product. Exposed to an inappropriate rationality that it seldom survives. Miles away from the true world of the consumer.

IF YOU HAVE SOMETHING IMPORTANT TO SAY, DON'T USE LONG SENTENCES

And in at least one out of three presentations with the added complication that, one more time, the beamer in the meeting room is not working and everyone is waiting with irritation for a technician to fix the thing. A little tip for advertisers:

SINCE HE'S ALREADY THERE,
LET THE TECHNICIAN
HELP TO DECIDE.
HE MIGHT BE THE ONLY ONE WITH NORMAL FEELINGS.

CHAPTER 4

CREATIVITY PAYS. BUT WHICH ONE OF THE TWO?
ABOUT THE EFFECT OF CREATIVITY

At the end of the year, strange things happen in medialand. Magazines that are usually able to get only modest fees for their ad space, due to limited circulation, experience an unexpected boost. Just flip through the pages of the last December issue of Lübeck's city magazine Piste. Or look at the last commercial blocks of the year on the small local TV station Hamburg 1. Chances are that you'll encounter great advertising that you've never seen before. And will never see again.

The crux of the matter is that ad agencies have to publish their most creative work somewhere to be eligible for competitions. And since clients are generally not inclined to support this kind of self-promotion, the agencies book these spots themselves.

In advertising, there are two kinds of creativity. Audience-oriented creativity that excites people and boosts market shares. And festival-oriented creativity that expert judges find new, courageous, and unusual.

A slightly more heretical way to put it would be "extrinsically motivated creativity" and "intrinsically motivated creativity."

CREATIVITY PAYS. BUT WHICH ONE OF THE TWO?

They overlap but are by no means identical. The momentum of an advertising idea is no guarantee for industry praise or awards. And equally, a flood of awards is no guarantee that a campaign will do its job in the marketplace. Ergo, there are advertisers who never manage to stand out as top-level creative forces, even if they create exciting campaigns and ignite momentum repeatedly. And there are also advertisers who are known for their top-level creativity and have never had a real smash hit.

A 2001 study published by the Technical University in Berlin analyzed the influence of creativity on the effectiveness of advertising (Trommsdorff et al., 2001). The researchers' main observation is that two opposing tendencies overlap in creative advertising: the more creative, i.e. unusual, the message, the more interesting, but also strange, is its effect on the audience. In other words:

TOO MUCH CREATIVITY
WILL DROWN POSITIVE MOTIVATION
IN NEGATIVE DIFFICULTY.

This is where the two types of creativity differ. Because this is where the naïve, unmotivated consumer differs from the ambitious, alert panel judge, who can be challenged with an exponentially higher degree of intellectual and motivational difficulty. And who reads a high degree of unusualness or difficulty as a sign of quality.

Award-winning creativity wraps its message in constructed symbolism, looking like a rebus puzzle.

CREATIVITY PAYS. BUT WHICH ONE OF THE TWO?

The effect is twofold and is like walking on the ridge of a mountain. On the one hand it must be assumed that most viewers in front of the television have neither the willingness nor the patience to solve the riddle. On the other, it can be assumed that those viewers who made an effort resulting in "I understand the message" have greater motivation. It's like grade school. What is drilled into you bounces off. What you learn for yourself sticks.

Jung was supposed to give a speech at a conference. The audience was highly attractive, all board members and marketing executives of big companies. Four speeches were already scheduled. The first: Adding value through creative advertising. The second: Excellent/Award-winning advertising is more effective. The third: Creativity makes advertising more efficient. The fourth: How to win creative awards and market success for the same reasons. To enrich this audience with a fifth speech about the two types of creativity was not easy, but it worked marvelously.

Announcing this difference publicly is probably the worst treason in the business. The self-congratulatory ad we published in the daily paper Die Welt after we won our Effies was equally provoking. Two skulls appeared with the headline:

"BEWARE OF ADVERTISERS
WHO ARE ONLY CHASING AWARDS FOR CREATIVITY."

The ad copy read: "Ad agencies are called the secret seducers. They are supposed to know sophisticated methods to influence, stimulate, seduce consumers. But they really seduce their clients.

CREATIVITY PAYS. BUT WHICH ONE OF THE TWO?

They blind them with medals, Golden Lions and the like. They pretend that creativity is the flight approach into market success. And clients gamely drop their advertising millions into the magic hat. But is creativity really a hard currency? Is it what makes an ad campaign effective? Or does it perhaps require a second, more unique talent?

Once a year, the Association of German Advertising Agencies, GWA, hands out a different kind of award: the Effie. It is the only competition where effectiveness wins over creativity. And thus exposes the vanity of some advertisers..."

Was it serious? Was it bold? Was it ironic? This ad furrowed the brows of our colleagues. But we didn't place that expensive double-page Welt ad for them.

Compare, if you will, seven minutes of a commercial block in Germany with seven minutes of a Cannes reel. You won't find many similarities. And you won't find more if you compare Cannes with British or American TV ads.

Cannes is an exhibition, an awards show with the emphasis on "show." Even high professional standards and the perfect festival organization can't change that.

Many of the displayed pieces had never been produced with real budgets. They are showpieces—like the many prototypes exhibited at auto shows. No motor under the hood. No registration sticker. Never been on the road. Or at least not in the form they are presented.

CREATIVITY PAYS. BUT WHICH ONE OF THE TWO?

Again and again, an attempt is made to connect advertising that wins awards with advertising that attracts customers. But this means walking on thin ice. Too often, creative competitions reward campaigns that fly right over the consumers' heads and don't trigger real momentum.

But award-winning campaigns more often miss the point than miss the consumer. Most frequently because the campaign idea determines the message instead of vice versa. Sure, a message driven by a specific market situation is harder to communicate than a message more or less chosen by the creative mind. One of the most creative campaigns of the past few years was a series of ads for a shoe store, in which the height of the heels is praised as the Unique Selling Proposition. But do you know any decent woman who bases her decision to buy a shoe on the height of the heel?

Of course, a panel judge who has dealt with advertising for decades will react differently to communication than someone who, unburdened by background information, browses through the pages of a magazine or sits in front of his TV.

IF YOU ASSUME
THAT THE MOST GRATEFUL AUDIENCE IS
INTELLIGENT, CURIOUS, AND ALREADY
SLIGHTLY GIDDY,
IT PROBABLY APPLIES MORE TO THE AVERAGE
PANEL JUDGE THAN TO THE
AVERAGE CONSUMER.

EBAY "MINE!" PRINT 2003:
WHAT MAKES EBAY UNIQUE? IS IT THE AMOUNT OF PRODUCTS OFFERED? THE WORLDWIDE TRANSPARENCY? THE PERFECT SYSTEM? OR IS IT THE THRILL OF BIDDING, THE EXCITEMENT OF FOLLOWING THE AUCTIONS, AND THE JOY OF WINNING? OUR CAMPAIGN FOCUSES ON THE EMOTIONAL EXPERIENCE. AND OUR SLOGAN GETS RIGHT TO THE CORE OF THAT EXPERIENCE: "THREE... TWO... ONE... MINE!"

CREATIVITY PAYS. BUT WHICH ONE OF THE TWO?

Twenty years ago, the Art Directors Club of Germany tried something spectacular. After the judging was over, they sent ten average Berliners through the exhibit to see where overlap or discrepancy occurred. The idea was soon buried, probably because it worked so well. The average Berliner remained perfectly average, even in the hallowed halls of the ADC. And found his own favorites.

Luckily, there is overlap between the two kinds of creativity. It is exactly the area where communication is new and unusual without posing too much of a challenge and clouding the intended perception.

At Jung von Matt, we are especially proud of having won not only the most Effies — the highest award for efficiency in advertising — over the past fifteen years, but also of being frontrunners in many creative competitions. But the question we most frequently have to answer is actually: Does creative advertising sell better? Does entertaining advertising sell better?

Does advertising that is popular with the audience sell better?

Many studies suggest this conclusion. But any attempt to derive a rule brings up an exception. A famous conclusion from advertising studies suggests that the degree of empathy for an advertising idea is inconsequential to its effectiveness. Housewives were polled about a laundry detergent campaign that was one of the most obnoxious TV annoyances of its time. Their verdict: the ad is terrible but the product is outstanding.

So this campaign had done its job. It managed to present this product as superior to the average consumer, who otherwise would not have been able to distinguish one from another. No attempt to sway the customer with a nice advertising idea. Thus it can be deduced that likeability in itself does not generate momentum. Advertising must be more than just nice.

The key to understanding audience-oriented advertising is understanding how recipients react to it. The answer to the question "Which kind of advertising works?" is "personal improvement." By personal improvement we mean everything that conforms to or comes close to personal ideals that match as nearly as possible the blueprints we all carry around with us.

Just as everyone has an idea of the perfect body, we believe that everyone carries a blueprint of his self-image with him. Advertising will be more effective if it serves this self-image, and will be less effective if it ignores or belittles this self-image. In a broad study about the relationship between creativity and effectiveness in advertising, Kover (et al., 1995) showed that recipients perceive advertising as being creative if it equals a contribution to their personal improvement — the personal ideal of self — or at least resembles it.

The conclusion is pretty simple:

FIRST OF ALL, THINK OF THE PERSON YOU WANT TO ADDRESS.

CREATIVITY PAYS. BUT WHICH ONE OF THE TWO?

Ski jumping provides a good representation of the mutual dependence of creativity and effectiveness. Judges give scores for style and distance. Those scores are gathered independent of each other. And, theoretically, it is possible that someone who jumps only 30 meters can achieve the highest score for style. Or the other way around, someone who sails almost all the way into the audience can fail stylistically.

But just as it is probable that someone with outstanding style will jump farther, it is also probable that a campaign with an excellent idea will sell more.

Where is the difference then? Festival-oriented creativity usually aims at the joy of decoding. This means, it maximizes the novelty factor and doesn't immediately reveal what it is driving at. This boosts curiosity and interest as well. Just like you approach an animal or a plant you don't know with curious interest.

What is most important is that the decoding is possible. And it should be fun, not work.

IF THE CONSUMER IS GIVEN TOO MUCH OF A MENTAL CHALLENGE, HE DROPS OUT.

You must have wondered more than once why the difficulty of most typical sweepstakes is usually on the following level. Please fill in: "First com_ first serv_."

The consumer will only stick with a puzzle he can solve easily. Our theory is that if the primary message is unambiguous, the secondary messages might as well be mysterious. It might even cause the viewer to want to see the ad several times. A certain mysteriousness can pique curiosity and lead to engagement and interaction.

In a commercial for Audi, the protagonist puts his briefcase down in a factory building. Soon afterwards the whole factory blows up. What was really nothing more than a dramaturgical error led to adventurous speculation. What was in the briefcase? The business partner's resignation? Or a competitor's plans? The mystery gave the spot almost cult status.

The spot was neither well made nor particularly popular, but it had momentum. It engaged the audience, it triggered something. Because the fun of decoding a message was accompanied by the pride of decoding it successfully. The mysterious, puzzling, hidden is more fascinating than the obvious. That's why we believe in the often mentioned pleasure of decoding. But it is like every other magic weapon—dangerous. Very tight is followed by very loose. If you challenge the consumers too much, you risk losing them.

We have to offer the consumer a game he is willing to participate in freely. One he keeps playing to the end, and during which he can't help but get the message by himself. Since every successful experience generates positive emotions, the sender of such a communication game will get an additional empathy bonus. Simply put:

CREATIVITY PAYS. BUT WHICH ONE OF THE TWO?

WITHOUT THE FUN OF DECODING,
THERE'S NO FUN IN ADVERTISING.

Decoding sounds complicated but it is actually common human behavior. Every one of us constantly perceives his social environment and evaluates others by analyzing and judging their behavior. And we use these perceptions to evaluate what is fun.

No socially intelligent person would think of calling himself well-liked in the presence of others. Particularly if he knows that the others don't like him very much. He will instead do things that will make him seem likeable in the others' eyes.

Of course, he has to find a stage that will give him exposure. If he is clever, appears to be authentic and not pretentious, his actions will be perceived as he intended. His behavior will be decoded, and he will be classified as likeable. Whether brand or person—if you are obnoxious and pretentious, people will refuse you. But if you communicate in an original and winning way, they will listen to you, they will want to believe you.

In one TV commercial, we set up a pseudo test in which we juxtaposed a kitchen sponge that has a scouring side with the cleaning power of a man. An attractive young man with a fashionable three-day stubble was literally tested against the sponge. A Ceran stovetop was scoured and wiped with his face. Then we showed what the sponge could do.

The young man could do nothing but lose and the sponge could do nothing but win. The fun of decoding won over reason. Sales increased significantly during the run of the TV commercial, even if the communication didn't offer any surprises per se.

A surefire mistake in communication is to under-challenge the consumer. Under-challenge doesn't generate momentum. We won't go as far as some advertisers who fight the stigma of the "dumb consumer" and demand intellectually sophisticated advertising. But we do believe that advertising has to be challenging. And contrary to Goebbels, who propagated that one should aim towards the lower end of the target group, we think we should aim at the upper end. Because every target group has idols it tries to emulate.

Advertising that is immediately understood by everyone has an intrinsic flaw. Build a motorbike that everyone can ride. Make a dress that every woman can wear.

HELLO BOREDOM!

When a man who didn't understand Pablo Picasso's paintings asked the artist if he could explain them to him, Picasso retorted, "Do you understand Chinese?" When the man said he didn't, Picasso said, "You see, art is just like the Chinese language. If you don't learn it, you won't understand it either."

The people we want to reach with advertising are not ignorant. They are simply not interested. They didn't buy the magazine to read any other content than the articles. They didn't turn on the TV to turn on their brain for something they didn't want to

RICOLA "FINNS," TV SPOT 1998:
"WHO INVENTED IT? THE SWISS. AND WHO EXACTLY? RICOLA."
THIS DIALOGUE WASN'T JUST MEMORABLE, LIKE A SLOGAN, IT
ALSO WON A GOLDEN EFFIE. THIS CAMPAIGN, ORIGINALLY CON-
CEIVED ONLY FOR THE GERMAN MARKET, IS NOW RUNNING ALL
OVER EUROPE. AND THE AMERICAN MARKET ADS ARE ALSO OURS.

DIRECTOR: MARTIN SCHMID AND CHRISTIANE BRUNNER-SCHWER
PRODUCTION: JO!SCHMID

CREATIVITY PAYS. BUT WHICH ONE OF THE TWO?

watch. Those who are kind enough to allow us to address them with our ads do it only under the condition that we entertain, not molest them.

Even if trend researchers dish up a new type of consumer every couple of months — human emotionality is a safe currency for future investments. That's why the big successes of the entertainment industry — movies, books, TV series, or music — are always based on the same human feelings and expectations.

However, decoding has its own boundaries in every culture. In Great Britain a successful campaign can have a decoding depth on the level of a semi-difficult rebus puzzle. Unthinkable for a broad German target group.

Scandinavian advertising has a special touch when it comes to portraying human foibles. In Italy, you'll do well with warm-heartedness. In the USA, decoding fun usually ends with the question "What's in it for me?" And for the French, we assume, the favorite kind of decoding is still unhooking a bra.

But, independent of the right dose of decoding, festival-oriented creativity has some validity in its own right.

Because every festival creates an atmosphere of competition, and therefore achievement. Without the Olympic games, no one would run 100 meters in less than 10 seconds. Only comparison with the best drives achievement. Only competition fuels ambition.

CREATIVITY PAYS. BUT WHICH ONE OF THE TWO?

WHAT MADE SAN GIMIGIANO ONE OF THE MOST BEAUTIFUL PLACES IN THE WORLD?

Competition. As a sign of their wealth, the competing families of the Tuscan nobility erected a total of 72 towers. "The higher the richer." Ambition knew no bounds, and thus they created the Manhattan of the Middle Ages.

One-upmanship doesn't just make towers higher, it also makes ideas better. And it is high time, since we face a digital age where media consumption becomes increasingly voluntary. In that world, the majority of ads we know today wouldn't stand a chance — too boring for the free man.

Our industry has advertising festivals for competition. Agencies that categorically don't participate in these festivals (a tempting thought considering the application costs: Jung von Matt pays out 500,000 euros every year!) have trouble keeping their creative talent.

And without talent there won't be any kind of creativity, not even audience-oriented.

We remember only too well the fall of a successful agency that, disappointed by a jury result, decided never to participate in a festival again. The corresponding press conference marked this agency's last grand flourish. It drowned in the anonymity of a functioning organization that manufactured ads as if they were screws.

CREATIVITY PAYS. BUT WHICH ONE OF THE TWO?

Antoine de Saint-Exupéry said, "If you want someone to build a ship, don't give him tools, awaken in him the longing for the ocean."

For creative people, this has to be modified. If you want someone to create a great campaign, awaken in him the longing for a Golden Lion.

Unfortunately, the two types of creativity have little respect for each other. The typical proponent of festival-oriented creativity laughs about Milka's violet cow. He thinks that "Joy Joy Joy" is too banal. And he won't see a groundbreaking idea in the term Gesundheitskasse (literally "health insurance," a twist on the actual German term Krankenkasse, "sickness insurance"). And the typical proponent of audience-oriented creativity smiles—albeit a little pained—about most medal winners.

At Jung von Matt we nurture a culture that takes both types of creativity seriously. Of course we are pleased with awards. But the highest honor is sitting in an ice-cream parlor, hearing two teens at the next table rave about the latest Ricola commercial that has never won a creative award—and never should.

All in all, both kinds of creativity have a right to exist not only on their own but also in combination, as a mixing board for the highest momentum. As surprising as possible but with a familiar point of reference. The absurd or crazy coded with familiar emotions, well-known situations, or familiar people in such a way that the consumer is challenged but never over-challenged.

The market value of many awards and the offers of many competitors have unfortunately prompted some of our creative people to turn their backs on Jung von Matt. But most of them left something behind. A campaign you like to watch again and again. Or an idea you won't ever forget.

During our semi-annual evaluation meetings, where all employees define their career goals, our art director Sergei Ivanov made an indelible impression. He wrote:

"MY GOAL IS TO SEE PEOPLE CRY FOR JOY
WHEN ONE OF MY TV SPOTS INTERRUPTS THEIR FAVORITE MOVIE."

We liked this sentence so much that we used it as the title of our competition show reel. And we included a Kleenex.

CHAPTER 5

SCRATCHES ARE SEXY, THE SWEAT OF FEAR ISN'T
ABOUT PROVOCATION IN ADVERTISING

When he was a child, von Matt had to attend forty, fifty plays with his parents. One stuck in his memory. When, after a few minutes, an actor screamed "You syphilitics!" at the audience, his parents left the theatre, outraged.

He stayed. And learned something he can use over and over again today. How provocation can offend some people and fascinate others. It may not be unusual to be provoked in the theatre these days. It was different in 1966, when Peter Handke's play "Offending The Audience" had its premiere in Zurich.

Who remembers the Prince of Homburg? He was a boxer for more than a decade. A butcher by trade, Norbert Grupe—that was his real name—was probably pretty clever, but certainly courageous, when he made television history as a guest on the Saturday night sports show Aktuelles Sportstudio. He didn't say a single word. Grupe answered every question with silence and a smile, delivering a rhetorical KO to moderator Rainer Günzler.

Was it his idea? Was it a dare? Was it cocaine? Was it an adviser who instructed him "The less you say the more intelligent you come off?" Si tacuisses, philosophus mansisses.

SCRATCHES ARE SEXY, THE SWEAT OF FEAR ISN'T

Or was it authentic speechlessness? Whatever—it was a masterpiece of provocation. At a time when there were no private TV stations and Aktuelles Sportstudio reached pretty much half the nation.

Or John Lennon. Many images of him will be remembered. One is indelible. When, in 1969, he and his wife Yoko Ono refashioned their honeymoon into a unique peace demonstration.

They literally went to bed in the Amsterdam Hilton for one week and called the press. They called their demonstration "hair peace, bed peace." The message—imagine the world stayed in bed for a week. There would be peace for a week and the world would know what it's like.

All examples from an era when people who provoked for the heck of it still had a name. In Germany, we called them—with contempt or admiration, depending on the individual point of view—Provos.

This suggests that provocation can also trigger high momentum in marketing communication. In many cases it is the only chance to really break through.

Provocation starts from this premise—that only the unusual, irritating, provoking can find its way into the consciousness of our target group, because the ordinary has no novelty value and doesn't set anything in motion.

George Bernard Shaw put it like this:

IF YOU DO NOT SAY A THING IN AN IRRITATING WAY, YOU MAY AS WELL NOT SAY IT AT ALL.

And Werner Kroeber-Riel says, "Since irritation goes hand in hand with activation, it enhances the mental and emotional processing and storage of an advertising message. ... The wooed recipients' defensive attitude related to irritation does, however, disturb the acceptance and persuasion effects of advertising, particularly the effects of advertising on the inner attitudes leading to purchase." (Kroeber-Riel/Esch, 2000, p. 174) But since activation is the bottleneck factor these days, provocation has become an indispensable stylistic tool.

If you want to provoke, you have two strategic options: the strategy of stimulation and the strategy of confrontation. The most explicit example of the strategy of stimulation can be witnessed in Hamburg's famous Herbertstrasse, a street in the red-light district where prostitutes sit in shop windows waiting for their clients. The women offering themselves there obviously dress to provoke. Do they do it because they like it? Because they feel most comfortable this way? Hardly. They are hard-selling themselves and use provocation to do it. No provocation = less business. The world's oldest profession has employed the latest advertising trend for a long time.

How can advertising itself be provoking? With provoking images, for example. We have used this stylistic tool again and again in our ad campaigns for the animal rights organization Noah.

Ihre Meinung zu BILD, sido?

DANKE FÜR DIE TITT'N

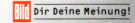

Bild Dir Deine Meinung!

BILD bedankt sich bei sido für seine ehrliche und unentgeltliche Meinung.
Übrigens: Über 1300 junge Frauen bewarben sich 2008 als BILD-Seite-1-Girl. Mehr Infos auf www.bild.de/fakten

BILD-ZEITUNG "CONFESSOR CAMPAIGN," INTEGRATED CAMPAIGN 2009: TESTIMONIAL CAMPAIGNS ARE CONVENTIONAL—BUT NOT WHEN THEY ENABLE CRITICAL OPINIONS. AND WHEN THE CLIENT, INSTEAD OF PAYING A FEE, DONATES € 10,000 FOR A GOOD CAUSE. THE CONFESSOR CAMPAIGN, FOR WHICH WE WERE ABLE TO ENLIST NUMEROUS CELEBRITIES, SUCH AS FORMER GERMAN FOREIGN MINISTER, HANS-DIETRICH GENSCHER, AND POPULAR RAPPER SIDO, BECAME THE MOST SUCCESSFUL IMAGE CAMPAIGN SINCE THE BEGINNING OF OUR PARTNERSHIP WITH BILD 20 YEARS AGO.

PHOTOGRAPHER: MATHIAS BOTHOR

One day, von Matt read in the paper that the EU indirectly sponsors bull fights because it sponsors cattle raising in Europe. That inspired the agency to produce a cinema spot. It showed brutal scenes in which toreros were attacked by bulls, and constructed the following provoking connection:

"EVERY DEAD TORERO CREATES A NEW JOB.

Is that why the EU sponsors bull fights?" Sometimes a single word that is completely out of place in the sacred Disneyland of advertising is enough to create a provoking effect.

When we took over the Bild account, one of the tasks was to develop a cinema spot. We asked ourselves, which force will create the strongest momentum for Bild in this youthful environment? The answer: openness when dealing with critics. No one thought this brand had the guts for this message. Adolescents least of all.

We filmed Nina Hagen giving her honest opinion of Bild. The idea had already astonished Nina. At first, she could hardly believe that we would actually pay her for her honest opinion of Bild. And she gave it to us with a particularly expressive "Shit!" Just as she uttered it, the viewer was prompted: Bild Dir Deine Meinung! [Form your own opinion!]

Compared to later cinema spots for Bild that got a lot of applause, this first spot left viewers perplexed. Everyone was baffled. The spot's radical openness silenced the audience. But the spot generated a momentum we have never achieved since.

To this day we can't believe that a newspaper that for more than 50 years refused to write out the word "Sh**" allowed it in their ad. A test of courage for Gert Borsum, who was responsible for the spot as Bild's Director of Communications. A year later, he was elected Client of the Year by the Art Directors Club.

Let's stay with soft particulars and hard facts for a moment. By far the most effective TV spot in 2001 was—according to the IMAS test of the leading trade magazine w&v—the "barfing flower" for our client Apollo-Optik. The goal was clear: to sell designer glasses at a reasonable price. We showed a young woman gazing dreamily at a fresh, blooming daffodil. When the flower finally notices the woman, looking homely in her unfashionable glasses, it turns sideways and throws up. In this spot, conventions are literally turned on their head.

It was not so easy to sell this idea to the client. But eventually he was convinced, and even encouraged us to make it look really green. And he didn't mean the lawn. The result was overwhelming. The spot wasn't simply noticed, it also created momentum on a hitherto unseen scale. During this spring campaign, new orders at Apollo-Optik were up more than 35%.

The content of advertising can be provoking too. In the early 1990s, the fashion brand René Lezard was faced with the problem that its high-end value wasn't recognized. Despite the highest levels of design and quality, René Lezard was never seen as a top brand but always a few levels below.

SCRATCHES ARE SEXY, THE SWEAT OF FEAR ISN'T

We were thinking, all fashion brands want to show their product in the ads. And all of them want to stress especially high quality in a wonderful mood and setting. To achieve this, they always use the same mechanisms. Ever better photographers. Ever more beautiful faces. Ever more exotic locations. The uniformity of products and concepts makes it more and more difficult to force a differentiation.

We recommended a straightforward approach and suggested the slogan:

"REGRETTABLY EXPENSIVE!"

Few fashion slogans caught on as quickly as this one. Although it was only shown in small print in ads and René Lezard had only a modest media budget, the entire fashion scene knew it by the end of the season. Regrettably, merchants' reservations were never overcome. The slogan was pulled after three years of creating quite a stir.

We achieved a similarly provoking effect with a detail of our Porsche campaign. We came up with the following idea. To underline the outstanding performance of these cars and the resulting responsibility placed on the owner, every Porsche ad was supposed to feature the sentence "Porsche recommends: Drive carefully!" It became the most discussed six point line of all time.

Other surefire tools for provocation are the often-quoted taboo topics for advertising: politics and religion. We hit the bull's eye several times with politics in particular. Three of the best were in the Sixt campaign.

Just before Gerhard Schröder was elected chancellor of Germany, the media blared about the uncertainty of his political course. We used that for a Sixt ad that promoted rental cars with a navigation system. It showed Gerhard Schröder looking to the left and right: "Sixt has cars for people who are not quite sure where they're headed."

When Oskar Lafontaine threw in the towel after a short stint in his government position, we placed an ad for Sixt-Leasing. It showed the newly appointed cabinet members with Lafontaine crossed out. The headline: "Sixt also leases cars for colleagues during their trial period."

The biggest and best coup we scored was with conservative-party chairwoman Angela Merkel. The first page of the ad showed Ms. Merkel with her much-discussed non-hairstyle and the headline: "Care for a new hairdo?" The second page showed her with a wind-tousled head: "Rent a Sixt convertible!"

The special twist was that the CDU chairwoman showed impressive good humor and played along. The Sixt ad and its echo in the press rewarded her with an unexpected wave of goodwill.

THE TYPICAL WIN–WIN SITUATION OF PROVOCATIVE ADVERTISING.

Sixt and Ms. Merkel were swept up in a media storm. All the big TV stations and newspapers reported it. Many of them with a picture of the ad on the front page. This created a media value of more than 3.2 million euros. From a two-title ad that cost less than 100,000 euros.

Sports or movie celebrities who employ their own marketing managers do not grant favors like that. It will definitely become expensive. Only media can afford to take this road, but it also can be a borderline case legally. For Bild, we ran a TV commercial with interview clips of famous sports figures for a year without admonishment or penalties. These were scenes from interviews where the athletes were at a loss for words and were only uttering long "uhhhms." The caption: "You can read what these athletes are trying to say in Bild."

The strategy of stimulation also includes advertising which, ironically, discriminates against a minority.

ONE FACT STANDS OUT: THE MINORITY THAT MOST OFTEN FEELS DISCRIMINATED AGAINST IS A MAJORITY— WOMEN.

More than half of the complaints received by the German Advertising Council are about hostility towards women. Sometimes with such absurd reasoning that would turn anyone against them. It is not always easy to understand what women don't like about this or that ad.

SCRATCHES ARE SEXY, THE SWEAT OF FEAR ISN'T

Von Matt would love to erase one evening from his memory when he had to defend a TV spot in front of outraged female CDU politicians on a talk show.

Women often feel misunderstood because they interpret content more emotionally than men. This means that a single message can trigger astonishingly different reactions in men and women.

A good example for this is an early date between Jung and his (now) wife. In a candlelit setting, he said to her "It took a thousand wrong turns to finally find you." His wife was melting away. No man had ever said anything so beautiful to her. But Jung simply wanted to say that he repeatedly took wrong turns on the way to the restaurant because his car's navigation system went totally crazy.

Once, however, one of our ads displayed hostility towards women that was so unmistakable that interpretation didn't come into play anymore. A Porsche with a big dent in the hood was parked at the intersection in front of our agency. One of our creative people took a picture and wrote the text "Sixt also rents to women." Mr. Sixt didn't place the ad until he had made sure that less than 5% of his customers were women.

The second type of provocation, the fighting strategy, is based on the principle that any competition attracts an audience. Manchester United against Bayern München. Schumi One against Schumi Two. Quiz master Günther Jauch against the contestant. Everybody is hooked. Everybody takes sides.

SATURN "CHEAP IS HOT," TV SPOT 2003:
> FOR DECADES, THERE HAD NOT BEEN A SLOGAN THAT WAS QUOTED AS OFTEN AND THAT HAD AS MUCH EFFECT AS "CHEAP IS HOT." AS TOKENS OF THIS APPRECIATION, WE RECEIVED AN EFFIE AWARD IN GOLD AND A EUROPEAN EFFIE AWARD IN SILVER. THE SLOGAN WAS ALSO CRITICIZED FOR CONTRIBUTING TO THE CONSUMERS' UNWILLINGNESS TO MAKE A PURCHASE. IN OUR OPINION, IT JUST PROVIDED A NAME FOR THE TREND.

PRODUCTION/ANIMATION: LAUENSTEIN LAUENSTEIN

SCRATCHES ARE SEXY, THE SWEAT OF FEAR ISN'T

Why else do Champions League, Formula One, and "Who wants to be a Millionaire?" rake in unbeatable shares? It isn't the beautiful moves. It isn't the colorful cars. It's the fight that generates high momentum.

Advertising can also use this effect and get attention through a staged fight. Or get additional goodwill if David challenges Goliath. The most widespread form is comparative advertising, officially permitted in Germany for some time but still burdened with so many restrictions that it is hard to use. But the following also applies:

ATTENTION IS GIVEN TO THOSE WHO DARE.

A typical fighting strategy was employed in the Sixt campaign. Most of all, this campaign is more aggressive than it seems at first sight. It is also the best example for our metaphor of the Trojan Horse. The Sixt advertising campaign was the ideal example for this image. It is cleverly packaged hard sell. Every ad and every airport poster contains a competitive price offer. But you don't notice that.

Von Matt took over the Sixt account in 1985. At that time, Sixt was still ridiculed in the rental car trade as a negligible entity. But a new fighting strategy made Sixt the superior market leader. And opened an entrance into the European market.

Even Mr. and Mrs. Sixt admit that their company's success would not have been possible without this advertising. But we must admit that this advertising would not have been possible without Regine and Erich Sixt, who not only support innovative, provoking ideas, but also have the courage to follow through with them.

It is indisputable that provoking advertising generates higher momentum. Nevertheless, it is rarely used. Its main problem is that the side effects are hard to calculate. Sure, at some point you learn from experience simply by using provocation again and again. But you can never be sure. Neither that the effect will actually happen, nor that the effect-annoyance ratio will turn out positive in the end.

We were often unsure about the consequences of provocative advertising. Even had divided opinions in one case. We were meeting a friend from Hannover for dinner. It was shortly after the Lower Saxony elections, which were the decisive turn for Schröder's Social Democrat Party (SPD) candidacy for chancellor.

Our friend had an idea. "Let's mobilize the Lower Saxons' pride in a Lower Saxon chancellor and place an anonymous double-page ad in all newspapers in the state." We asked him who would pay the roughly 500,000 euros that it would cost. He answered "I will."

Jung was against this ad, since he greatly values the political neutrality of the agency. Von Matt was for it, because he loved the idea. Jung went on vacation, and the ad was placed. It showed the last four German chancellors with the caption "No Lower Saxon." Below was the headline "The next chancellor must be a Lower Saxon." We applied some communicative leverage here that wasn't available to the SPD, since the party hadn't yet agreed on Schröder as their candidate.

The ad, and the subsequent clear election victory, triggered a "fantastic" (von Matt) and "devastating" (Jung) run on the agency that was the only visible connection to the ad. Everybody wondered who was behind it. Wild speculations abounded. Since we were Audi's agency at the time, it was assumed that Wolfsburg had given the order. The press tried anything and everything to uncover this ad's origin, and several months later they found out.

What did the ad achieve? Since we left out smaller electoral districts on purpose, we could trace the results fairly precisely. In those electoral districts, Schröder was about 1.8 percentage points below his total result. A higher momentum than Jung was comfortable with.

We also remember cases where we could predict for our client what added value provoking advertising would generate. We were never as dead on as for the "Fulda" TV spot for e-Sixt. For this spot, we considered every little extraneous thing. And with great accuracy.

We were putting together a TV commercial for e-Sixt's online air travel program that was supposed to generate many clicks. Our idea was to present a city as the most depressing city in Germany. And e-Sixt as its citizens' last hope to fly out of there economically.

SCRATCHES ARE SEXY, THE SWEAT OF FEAR ISN'T

We just needed to find a suitable city to play the victim. We didn't want to pick an East German city, nor one of those cliché-laden towns like Mannheim, Castrop-Rauxel, or Salzgitter. Offenbach was out too, since Jung von Matt had an office there. Because von Matt once had a very unpleasant experience in Fulda—a lengthy car repair—we picked Fulda. The last important factor was that the Sixt branch in Fulda didn't bring in much business.

We presented the spot to Sixt and predicted that, after about ten days of air play the media would be full of news such as "A city fights for its reputation," etc. And that's exactly what happened. TV stations ZDF, SAT.1, and RTL, as well as countless newspapers and magazines from the Süddeutsche to Focus, reported on it. The Munich paper TZ put up a poster at thousands of its vending cases that read "Excitement about cheeky Sixt ad." For one week, the phone lines between Fulda, Pullach, and Hamburg were running hot. The most frequent question:

WHY FULDA?

We knew that the car breakdown would not be very exciting for the press, so we tried to come up with a more attention-grabbing story to exploit the excitement even more. Our former creative director Oliver Voss thought up the following story. He, who created the spot, was on vacation in Naxos eleven years ago. One evening he met a beautiful girl: Anna from Fulda. They spent the night on the beach, but the next morning she had to catch the ferry.

RWE "ENERGY GIANT," ENTERPRISE FILM 2009:
ELECTRICITY SUPPLIERS OFTEN GET STUCK WITH THE UNFLATTERING LABEL "ENERGY GIANT." BUT IT IS THE GIGANTIC SIZE OF AN ENERGY ENTERPRISE THAT ACTUALLY MAKES MANY PROJECTS AND INVESTMENTS POSSIBLE. THAT IS WHY RWE WAS TURNING THIS PROBLEM ON ITS HEAD: "IT CAN BE SO EASY TO MAKE BIG THINGS HAPPEN WHEN YOU'RE A GIANT." THIS IS THE GIANT'S MESSAGE THAT WAS ORIGINALLY CREATED FOR THE COMPANY'S EMPLOYEES. DUE TO ITS CONCISE NATURE AND POPULARITY, THE GIANT QUICKLY FOUND ITS WAY TO THE WEB AND GARNERED A LOT OF ATTENTION—ALSO FROM THE ENVIRONMENTAL ORGANIZATIONS, WHICH MANIPULATED

SCRATCHES ARE SEXY, THE SWEAT OF FEAR ISN'T

As they said goodbye she asked him to come to Fulda on the first Sunday in April. She would pick him up at the train station. Voss went, she wasn't there. For hours, he wandered aimlessly through the chilly city and swore to himself:

FULDA, YOU'RE GONNA PAY FOR THIS.

The press loved the story. One magazine even printed a sketch of the phantom Anna.

Meanwhile, excitement in Fulda was growing as well. Chief mayor Dr. Alois Riehl wrote to us. Cordially, but determined, he asked for restitution. We wrote a spot that presented Fulda as Germany's most beautiful city. And announced the first airing in all of Fulda's daily papers.

Even in this case there were only winners in the end. A city nobody ever talks about could present itself as a baroque attraction. Sixt could demonstrate to the audience, with great effect, that the company did more than just rent cars. The press had something to sink their teeth into. And — OK — our agency was mentioned as well.

Of course, provoking advertising has its limits. Precisely where provocation is exposed as senseless gawking. The consumer doesn't want any part in this. Because he recognizes the intention and it annoys him. Even provocation has to be relevant. Promoting chewing gum with a skull only makes sense if it is a chewing gum with particularly long-lasting flavor.

SCRATCHES ARE SEXY, THE SWEAT OF FEAR ISN'T

Frequently, the stylistic tool of provocation does not fit the character of the advertised product. Particularly when the brand is supposed to create confidence, like in ads for pharmaceuticals. Or investment vehicles. In these cases, provocation is like a highly potent drug that must be administered in exact dosage.

Provocation should only feel like a light tickle, not a heavy pounding. Long-term provocation requires a steadily growing dosage and is doomed to fail. Benetton did a disservice to our industry in this regard, when the campaign went overboard and pushed provoking advertising into a bad light. The Benetton campaign is provocation for provocation's sake. It had an extremely high attention value but a low activation value. It didn't achieve the tie-in between the provocation and the product.

We organized a big party for our 10th anniversary. It was supposed to be a "bad-taste party" with appropriately tasteless invitations. We designed a colorful fold-up — risqué pictures and randy text on cheap paper.

Never before had we caused such outrage. Our phones were ringing off the hook. Most clients and journalists were so pissed off that they sent their regrets. Jung decided to apologize for the tastelessness of the writing, which made things even worse.

But isn't it fitting that we not only demand that our clients have courage but also — after ten years — prove to have some ourselves?

CHAPTER 6

WHY RIGHT ADVERTISING IS WRONG
ABOUT THE CORRELATION BETWEEN STRATEGY AND CREATIVITY

When our agency was only a few weeks old, Jung stood before one of our first clients and argued desperately for an idea, the strength of which might not have been obvious. He was looking for examples and spontaneously came up with: "Look, Mr. Huffmann, this ad works just like the Trojan horse, wrapped up prettily on the outside so that the consumer is willing to let it come closer, but there's a hard sell inside."

He convinced the client and has been using this simile ever since. When von Matt heard it for the first time he loved it, and the Jung von Matt advertising philosophy was born:

GOOD ADVERTISING IS LIKE
THE TROJAN HORSE.

For more than ten years the Greeks tried to rescue Helen from Troy. But the city seemed invincible. The walls were too strong to overtake the city from the outside. Cutting off all supplies to the city didn't work either. And there was no psychological way to make the Trojans surrender.

Only a ruse could create the necessary momentum. The attackers appeared to retreat and left behind a present—the famous Trojan horse. Its wooden belly hid 30 of the most courageous Greek warriors. The Greeks got into the city, and Troy fell.

The Trojan horse is a highly effective idea. Otherwise, the Trojans would not have pulled it inside the city walls. And a compelling strategic ploy. Otherwise, Troy would never have been conquered. The original definition of strategy—strategy equals war stratagem or tactical trick.

To work strategically means to construct and execute a plan that can account for all future strategies and actions of the opponent and all possible influential factors. And using cunning to solve all the problems arising on the way to the goal.

Does this apply to typical marketing and communications strategies as well? Are advertisers gleefully constructing ruses to solve seemingly insurmountable problems and reach ambitious goals?

IN MARKETING COMMUNICATIONS RULES ARE TAKEN MORE SERIOUSLY THAN RUSES.

The basic checklist of marketing rules dictated by company policies, which should take everything into account that could influence communications. Precautions that, instead of a clear strategic solution, serve the purpose of assuring that nothing was left out.

Strategy is a big word. Often bigger than life. If it is said aloud in a meeting, everybody freezes and prays for a messiah to lead the way. But one has to be aware that strategy is often just a tool for the weak. Strategy can help achieve high momentum despite a product's inferior firepower. This is important for those who can't make it on sheer firepower alone.

A superior boxer doesn't need strategy—he simply has to apply his skills after the first gong. A superior racecar driver doesn't need strategy either—he just has to drive the fastest heat and then win the race from the pole position.

If your favorite soccer team has great rapport, fights their battles well, scores goals easily, and has a goalkeeper who is more than just a fly swatter, your team has everything it takes to win a game. The rest is pure luck.

On the other hand, our home team, FC St. Pauli—a team we feel close to since our offices are located in Hamburg's St. Pauli district—couldn't stay in the major league even with star strategist Ottmar Hitzfeld as coach.

STRATEGY IS POWERLESS
IF THE SUBSTANCE IS WEAK.

How ridiculous does it seem when, in a sport where luck can decide a game, there are extensive TV discussions about the real reasons for the defeat. And celebrations of the supposed ingenius strategy for victory.

> STRATEGY IS A WORD THAT IS RESPECTED BY EVERYONE.
> EVERYWHERE IT APPEARS, IT INSPIRES AWE.

In sports as well as in brand management. Rightfully so?

GOOGLE "HEAT MWC," APP 2011: HOW DO YOU LEAD THE WORLD'S MOBILE PHONE EXPERTS TO THE HOTSPOTS OF THEIR LARGEST INDUSTRY EVENT, THE MOBILE WORLD CONGRESS? OUR APP SHOWED THEM IN REAL TIME WHERE THE MOST CONGRESS PARTICIPANTS WERE AT ANY TIME — AT WHICH PRESENTATION, IN WHICH EXHIBITION HALL, OR, AT NIGHT, AT WHICH BAR. THE APP WAS DOWNLOADED MORE THAN 11,000 TIMES DURING THE 4 CONGRESS DAYS!

WHY RIGHT ADVERTISING IS WRONG

Still, the most important factor for strategy is firepower, the product itself. A superior product, such as a Mercedes-Benz or a BMW—completely independent of strategy—triggers desire. The better engine, the road action, the manufacturing quality, the all-round perfection are the decisive factors for market success. And, by no means least, the fact that the basic car is priced slightly lower than the competition.

If a product is not competitive, the best strategist in the world won't be of much help. On the other hand, a competitive product will always have a good chance independent of a good strategy.

We don't want to make a case for scrapping strategy altogether. Of course, clever ideas are necessary to position products and to find a competitive price and the right target audience. We simply want to correct the relationship between product and strategy. In favor of the factor that creates the highest momentum—the hard currency of "product."

Even in a time when product features are becoming increasingly similar, marketing is not everything. We're not the only ones with this opinion. After all, it is one of Proctor & Gamble's principles to advertise only those products with a clear market advantage. And Unilever has distilled its 1,600 brands to a marketable palette of only 400.

In advertising, it is the creative product that makes or breaks a campaign. There are many strategically correct ad campaigns. But a strategic stringency by itself does not create an effect.

It is just the approach path for a campaign's success. It is not success itself.

In our career, we've seen many, many botched creative presentations. But hardly ever a botched strategic presentation. Strategy is actually a rather more banal achievement than creativity, since it can be derived from objective facts and doesn't spring from sheer inspiration.

A true strategic achievement doesn't dazzle you with thoroughness and diligence but with consistency and courage. It's not about coming up with the most possibilities that would guarantee a positive message, but about concentrating on the one message that will be most promising. Because it uses the most ruses.

Strategy has become more than just the magic word of our industry; it is also its most basic instrument. The "copy strategy" is the new packing slip for the product manager.

From positioning the brand and determining the competition, i.e., the sources of business, to defining the target audience and the physical and psychological use value for the consumer as well as finding justifications for the use of the product and the campaign's tonality: everything is part of it, everything is under control, everything can be checked off. These days, all of these assessment tools have been adopted by women's magazines, which offer them for their readers' career planning. This self-thematization sells better with handy buzzwords borrowed from up-to-date management terminology like "ego marketing" or "self worth."

WHY RIGHT ADVERTISING IS WRONG

And all of it is correct—as long as the decisive strategic question is answered. What is the main issue? What should communication concentrate on?

But even in those cases where precise strategic paths are prescribed the decision about the right communication cannot be made by checking off the points mentioned above.

Is 5% more fruit content a ruse to become market leader in the densely populated field of fruit yogurts? Is it a ruse that relies on the same old clichés, that people have basically the same recurring needs and act accordingly, like Pavlov's dogs?

EVERY DECISION
ABOUT COMMUNICATION
HAS TO BE ABOUT FINDING
THE PATH OF SUCCESS THROUGH
UTMOST INSECURITY
AND FICKLE TASTE.

And decision-makers have to win emotional security and trust. But is it possible to judge which creative idea will trigger a focused impact—a.k.a. momentum—simply by arming yourself with the copy strategy?

When we were given the task of reviving Bluna, the cult orange soda of the 1970s, there was a danger of presenting its cult status, a decisive differentiating feature, in the wrong light.

Because how do you say "I am a cult brand" without sounding ridiculous? And creating exactly the opposite impression? Cult brands have an intrinsic "secret" character and do not become cult brands using the usual means of classic advertising. Our ruse consisted in leaving the beaten path and not proceeding according to the traditional wisdom of "Say what you are—show what you say."

On the contrary. This cult soda for young people was given two loony older gentlemen for protagonists, telling each other pseudo-logical stories about the different Bluna products. In such a way that you thought twice about the absurd logic the two were using.

Adding the slogan "Aren't we all just a little bit Bluna?" we continued the campaign from the point where the brand had its first success—the flower power peace movements of the early 70s. Although we had a small budget and we had to concentrate on radio spots, the slogan caught on quickly and became a frequently quoted phrase.

Just a few months after the start of the campaign, we noticed a fan's banner at a Grand Slam tournament that read "Aren't we all just a little bit Boris?" We knew then that the slogan had landed where a good slogan is supposed to. It wasn't what people once said, it was what people say now.

The biggest mistake in marketing communications is to transfer strategic marketing goals directly to strategic communication goals. This is called:

"ILLUSTRATED MARKETING."

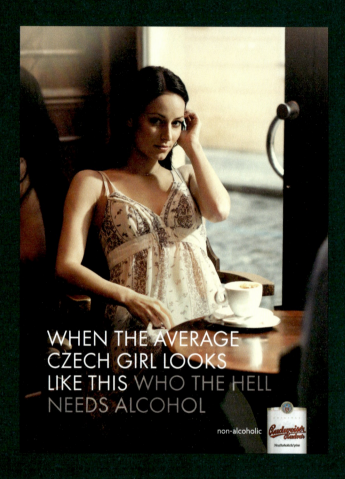

BUDWEISER BUDVAR "ALCOHOL FREE," ADVERTISEMENTS 2011:
KASPEN/JUNG VON MATT IN PRAGUE TAKES CARE OF BUDWEISER BUDVAR, ONE OF THE WORLD'S MOST FAMOUS BEERS. FOR THE ALCOHOL-FREE VERSION OF BUDWEISER WE DEVELOPED A VERY UNUSUAL PROMISE. OUR CAMPAIGN IS BASED ON THE WELL-KNOWN REPUTATION THAT THE CZECH REPUBLIC IS FULL OF BEAUTIFUL WOMEN. SUCH TYPICAL POSITIVE SIDE EFFECTS OF ALCOHOL AS "DRINKING THEM PRETTY" ARE NOW NO LONGER NECESSARY.

PHOTOGRAPHER: MIRO MINAROVYCH

WHY RIGHT ADVERTISING IS WRONG

Even if refined consumer and target group research seduces us to deliver tailored advertising to individual target groups that supposedly want it. You'll have to come up with something a little bit better to make them learn the content.

No matter what medium you choose. No matter how ubiquitous you are. No matter which lifestyle frames your presentation. Only a captivating story that presents the sender in a likeable way, and that is surprising and engaging, can anchor the message convincingly.

This insight comes at the end of era during which society's approach to advertising has been anything but relaxed. Jung's first personal confrontation with advertising came in a German Literature class, in a paper on Vance Packard's "The Hidden Persuaders."

Of course, he was outraged by these manipulations, and took an ambitious stance. He was 15 years old. And, as the Italian philosopher, historian, literary scholar, and politician Benedetto Croce once put it, those who have not been socialists before their 30th birthday have no heart. Those who are still socialists after their 30th birthday have no sense.

The only politically correct, and therefore acceptable, advertising at the time was a straightforward presentation of the product's use value. As a result, the great lingering fear of failure for advertisers and their clients was centered in communicating the content. In other words, in digging up, or making up, the message. And less frequently within the creative communication process!

WHY RIGHT ADVERTISING IS WRONG

"What" was more important than "How."

A fact that also became apparent during the shaping of the classic "copy strategy." Depending on the company and personal experience, great importance was placed on determining a serious and tangible definition of the target group, the product's use value, and all arguments supporting credibility. And not much on a precise analysis of the competition.

Military wisdom says that any battle plan becomes outdated after the first contact with the enemy. The same holds true for marketing communication.

EVERY STRATEGY HAS TO BE READJUSTED AS SOON AS THE COMPETITION ENTERS THE MARKETPLACE.

In real life, this flexibility is rare. This is mainly due to the hierarchical position of communication tasks within an organization. When a strategy has been approved on the top floor, everybody clings to it all the way down.

But it is due even more to the fact that the competition and their achievements are taboo subjects for many manufacturers. A blatant error, because misjudging the competition leads to approaches that are completely wrong.

Classic copy strategy does not explicitly consider this "competition for awareness"—this vying for the holiest and most desirable object of today's advertising world, the attention and

Ist es nicht ungerecht, daß Ihr Müll immer Mercedes fährt und Sie nicht?

Einen günstigen Mercedes und dazu noch 500 Lufthansa Meilen: Das kriegen Sie bei Sixt. Buchen Sie unter Telefon: 0 89 / 66 69 50.

SIXT RENT A CAR "GARBAGE TRUCK," PRINT 1993:
HEADLINE: "IT'S JUST NOT FAIR, IS IT? YOUR TRASH GOES MERCEDES AND YOU DON'T?"
ONE OF MORE THAN A HUNDRED VARIATIONS OF THE RECURRING THEME: MERCEDES AT A BARGAIN PRICE. THE SIXT ADS ARE PROTOTYPES FOR OUR METAPHOR OF THE TROJAN HORSE. THEY COME ALONG AS A NICE PACKAGE BUT ALWAYS CONTAIN A CONCRETE OFFER.

interest of the target group. There would not just be a Source of Business but also a Source of Potential Interest, for example.

And one component of the copy strategy would gain noticeably more attention and more serious treatment: tonality.

SUPERIOR, DYNAMIC, CONVINCING, LIKEABLE, MODERN, OPEN.

No, this is not a personal ad in the "Frankfurter Allgemeine Zeitung;" it is the typical tone a brand product manager takes in a briefing.

It's always shocking how superficial the definition of tonality is, how thoughtlessly a few terms are scribbled down that have only one purpose—not hurting anyone, not scaring anyone, not provoking contradictions. In short, not taking a stance.

What brand wants to appear inferior, undynamic, unconvincing? Truly goal-oriented terms for creative work are those whose opposites also make sense. For example: loud or soft, trendy or traditional, matter-of-fact or playful. Both poles make sense in terms of tonality.

But how can you tell at this stage of development which direction the creative team will think and work towards? That's why you choose hazy terms that are connected with the target group's consumer habits and lifestyles in some way. And that by no means restrict or hinder the creative team.

But how significant is tonality, really?

A comparison: it is easy to give concrete examples for "benefit" or "reason-why." You can reach for any number of experiences and examples. And immediately make references to the corresponding products from the competition.

It is relatively easy to talk about the usefulness of one's own product, elevating oneself high above all others. Insofar as the product actually has the famous "uniqueness" factor.

Which is rarely the case nowadays. The classic Unique Selling Proposition seems to have become extinct. Differentiation—advertising's primary goal per se—is nearly impossible in the field of rational product use value.

And even the famous characteristic Quality is not worth mentioning anymore. Quality and manufacturer or dealer warranties are already a conditio sine qua non for anyone entering a market.

There is often only one opportunity for differentiation—through communication. The possibilities for differentiating product use value are finite; the possibilities for differentiating product presentation are infinite. Or, in Picasso's words:

WHY RIGHT ADVERTISING IS WRONG

THERE ARE MANY TRUTHS.
BECAUSE IF THERE WERE ONLY ONE,
IT WOULD NOT BE POSSIBLE
TO PAINT A HUNDRED DIFFERENT PICTURES
OF THE SAME SUBJECT.

This makes tonality the main driving force for copy strategy in today's saturated competitive markets. And it is precisely the opportunity for uniqueness. Sure, no advertiser wants to miss out on the thematic security of product usefulness. Every piece of communication must have its story, every product its use.

But product use is generally no longer the feature that makes a product unique, desirable, and attractive. Product use can be easily duplicated by the competition. Just think about the many innovative ideas presented at the international technology fair, CeBIT. Once shown, soon everyone offers them. Maybe everyone hit upon the same idea at the same time...

So, it is not functional use value that binds a customer to a brand. It is rather the emotional ties the brand can establish with its customers. An emotional connection created by how the brand communicates with consumers.

At its core, professional (mass) communication doesn't work any differently than normal human communication. Just think about it for a second. What do people around you talk about, in general? Always about world affairs? Does everyone you cherish personally, to whom you feel close, always have something new to offer or say?

Hardly. In general, most people are the same. They talk a lot or a little. They drink a lot or a little. They gesticulate a lot or a little. They laugh a lot or a little. And they all talk about the same things. The current topics of the day. Politics, society, gossip, sports, TV, movies, music, etc. What are the big topics in Bild, on the evening news, etc.? No big surprise, since the media are nothing more than a mirror of public interest. They didn't invent human interests from scratch, did they?

So, why is communication with those with whom you have emotional ties so different and so exciting, if it isn't the novelty aspect of the conversation?

It is the personal way your loved ones and friends deal with things. The way they express themselves. The way they approach things. Whatever makes each person whole. That's what makes every individual so unmistakable. So you recognize him immediately, even if he looks completely different, after a haircut, a tanning session, or a visit with a personal trainer, for example. Even if he believes he has become someone else.

That is what is meant by tonality, that is the power of tonality. A tonality that triggers real momentum.

And that is what elevates successful brands above common products. Even if the generic version fares better in blind tests or similar quality checks, nobody buys it. Nobody likes it better than the original.

WHY RIGHT ADVERTISING IS WRONG

Speaking of originality. The authenticity of brands—whatever makes them original—depends directly on whether their intrinsic communicative values have substance. Or whether they are only things and nothing else. Whatever you make reality becomes reality.

A good example of this is Sixt. The brand's first notable success came with the message "Drive a Mercedes 190 for the price of a Volkswagen Rabbit." The breakthrough came with the offer "Drive First Class, Pay Economy." Consolidation through a constant barrage of innovations. Fully-equipped, premium cars as standard. Porsche 911, Harley-Davidson, all new Mercedes models for everyone—and affordable. Cell phones in your rental car, car rentals at ATMs, navigation systems, and e-Sixt. Sixt was always the first to offer these services. Or at least they announced them the loudest.

Sixt advertising always had a consistent appearance. The Sixt look, from small print ads to airport promotions, flyers and rear-view mirror accessories to the office chair at the counter.

All of this works as a whole but doesn't explain Sixt's communication success. Even more so, since the brand shed its look three times over the years. The real power lies deeper, in the ever surprising, provoking tone of aggressor in pricing and special offers.

While it has become chic to rent your car at Sixt, the brand Sixt has remained exciting, with outlaw appeal. Without that, the competition's numerous product offensives would have seriously hurt the brand.

WHY RIGHT ADVERTISING IS WRONG

As a Sixt customer, you automatically acquire a bit of cleverness. You are as self-confident, fresh, gutsy, and uninhibited as the brand itself. This is the result of communication—the tonality has always remained true to itself. And along with it, the brand has remained true to itself as well. That's how it became an original, a brand with an unmistakable profile.

And here's the challenge for all of us in the future: the creation, careful construction, and steady care of a brand that goes beyond the physical features of the product.

Communications strategy has thus advanced from a marketing sub-strategy to become a driving strategic force that—within the marketing mix—makes the decisive contribution in developing the uniqueness of brands. And tonality has evolved from wallflower to differentiating factor number one.

But all of these insights provide no magic remedy. Checklists alone are no guarantee of success—they only help us avoid mistakes. They are the "training wheels" of marketing, which we will discuss at length in Chapter 10.

CHECKLISTS MAY EVEN BE DANGEROUS.
BECAUSE THEY CONVEY A
TREACHEROUS SECURITY
AND OFTEN BLOCK THE VIEW
OF THE ESSENTIAL.

An extreme example is the crash of Swissair flight 111 over Halifax. Suddenly, there was smoke in the cockpit. If the pilot had followed his instincts, he would have immediately gone into a steep dive and saved the plane and, more importantly, the passengers. But he followed his head and lost precious time going through the checklist required in case of a fire.

You too have to follow your instincts in the merciless battle to the death between brands. And you will get no help from mechanical formulas or strategies for success.

On the contrary. Anyone who tries to recreate a proven brand success story with his own brand will never step out of the shadow of the original. Or, to stress it again, those who drive the ideal line will never be able to pass — even if the ideal line is the fastest way around a winding course.

Whether the chosen line of attack was the right one will only become apparent at the end of the race. But then the whole thing will be celebrated as a strategic victory! Just as Dr. Wolfgang Armbrecht, former head of marketing at BMW Germany, likes to say, "Strategy is the description of reality after the fact — at least if it went well!"

CHAPTER 7

THE BEST STRATEGISTS ARE LAZY GENIUSES
ABOUT THOSE WHO ARE SUPPOSED TO LEAD THE WAY FOR THE CREATIVE ONES

When Jung is offered a double-breasted blazer at the haberdasher's, he usually says, "That's not me." He doesn't say, "I don't like that." Or, "I don't need that." But, "That's not me." When we suggest an idea to a client, we sometimes hear, "That's not Mercedes-Benz." Or, "That's not Wella."

Does that mean the idea is wrong? Or is that why it's right? Is a double-breasted blazer really unbecoming on Jung? Or would it actually suit him better than those Richard James suits he always wears? Would he perhaps radiate more competence? Or more decisiveness?

As we mentioned briefly in the second chapter, communication is certainly a way to affirm an image, but even more it is a focused way to change, improve, and sharpen it. Communication is the force that must generate high momentum, not just an approving nod. If communication only had to secure an existing image, it would usually not be worth the money spent.

Our usual skepticism about pre-tests is kicked up a notch if the question comes up, "Does this idea fit the brand?"

If consumers view the post office as not very customer-oriented, an advertising concept with the mission to change that perception must NOT fit the brand. It must create a contradiction.

Of course, this contradiction—like everything in advertising—must be well measured and must not create a rift. It must be at the very limit of believability but never go beyond it. Right at the limit it can create the highest momentum; beyond it, it will have as much of an effect as someone shouting in the desert.

To get better control over what drives a brand image in the right direction and what simply drives media money, our industry invented Strategic Planners. Those responsible for analysis and planning of brand messages.

We advertisers are special among the creative crowd because we have the most demands and restrictions, and because our creativity has to be oriented towards a target audience.

WE ARE BEING PAID
TO DEAL WITH TARGET CONFLICTS.

How much freedom writers or sculptors have compared to us! That's why creative advertisers can only be those who "shoot a goal in a narrow space," as they say in soccer, those who don't need a lot of room to score.

As a creative person, Jung feels lost in the great wide world of freedom. Even in school he had a hard time when the teacher made him choose a composition topic himself. Those were hard hours for him because he needs the challenge of a defined problem to harness his creativity. He blossomed when a teacher gave him a topic such as "The griping old geezer in the modern world." This kind of necessity was the mother of his invention.

In an ad agency, many creative people work with more motivation towards their goal when they are given narrow parameters, whether the limits come directly from the client or from a strategic planner.

Some prefer to start in the dark and produce their first ideas from the gut. But when it comes to judging those ideas, it takes someone who can shed light on and look at those ideas with his head.

However, the strategic planner is only helpful when his work is precise. You need to be able to trust him blindly. Because if you can't, you will always have to check up on him. He'll just be in the way.

COMMUNICATION
IS LIKE A TRAIN TRACK.
IF YOU SET THE FIRST SWITCH WRONG
YOU WILL END UP FAR FROM YOUR DESTINATION,
EVEN IF ALL THE OTHER SWITCHES ARE SET CORRECTLY.

If a planner provides tight analysis and draws the right conclusions he can save you a lot of time and effort. And time is an important factor in the creative process.

CARITAS "ONE MINUTE OF SILENCE," ONLINE EVENT 2010:
TO ASSIST THE EARTHQUAKE VICTIMS IN HAITI, WE DEVELOPED A SONG, IN COLLABORATION WITH UNIVERSAL MUSIC, THAT COULD BE DOWNLOADED FOR THE CUSTOMARY RATES.
TITLE: ONE MINUTE OF SILENCE FOR HAITI.
CONTENT: 60 SECONDS OF SILENCE THAT WAS HEARD BY MANY AND REACHED A COMPLETELY NEW GROUP OF DONORS.

THE BEST STRATEGISTS ARE LAZY GENIUSES

In practice, the problem lies in the fact that planners and creative teams have to start at the same time, even though the creative team actually depends on the finished plan. Strategic planning and creation often get off to a parallel start but at some point begin to synchronize. Creation starts based on the client briefing, often without a narrowly defined strategy. Strategy starts at the same time and digs into the whole case. Creation starts more or less unburdened, then the two meet and grow closer until they hit the right path.

ORGANIZING THE CREATIVE PROCESS
WHILE LEAVING SPACE FOR CREATIVE CHAOS
THAT WILL YIELD A USABLE RESULT
AT THE RIGHT TIME
IS ONE OF THE GREATEST CHALLENGES
FOR AN AD AGENCY.

The prerequisite for excellent creativity is single-mindedness. And the main effect of good planning is single-mindedness. Unfortunately, this kind of one-track thinking relies on the willingness to make sacrifices. You have to let go of messages, something a client does only reluctantly. "It won't hurt if we add the latest results from Consumer Reports, our recommended retail price, and our phone number here, right?" Yes, it hurts the momentum.

Particularly here in Germany, people have a hard time concentrating on the essentials. We are proud of correctness and completeness. Of our Brockhaus encyclopedia and our Duden dictionary. In management classes, quantity is the holy mantra:

those who want a lot must demand a lot. But in communications, a modest approach gets you more.

THOSE WHO WANT A LOT MUST DEMAND VERY LITTLE.

Why? Very simple. Demanding a lot only works with subordinates. In communication, however, you're dealing with free people who decide on a whim whether they will meet your demands.

For these reasons, strategic planning has become an important discipline in advertising. According to Karen Heumann, co-founder of the German Planners Association, this discipline has become the third pillar of the ad agency business.

We used to believe that the ideal planner is creative. Even if he is not predestined for a strategist's job by his talent and training, even if he is a second-rate planner from the start, he has an advantage that is vital for collaboration between planning and creation—inevitably, his work takes both sides into account. Everything flows from one brain.

Strategy and creation are most naturally integrated when they come from one and the same source. There is no break between analysis and imagination, no kinked line, rather a hard-wired connection. This is how most creative agencies have been working for years, with strong creative personalities who integrate both functions.

THE BEST STRATEGISTS ARE LAZY GENIUSES

Today we are of a different opinion. The ideal planner is a planner. One of the reasons is that the creative job has become so demanding that there is no time left for developing strategies. Good creative people are rare. You have to direct their energy toward what no one else can do instead—producing creative ideas. More than ever, the creative person has to focus on creating and delegate the planning. This inevitably means that the strategic planner has to work for the creative guy. He has to subordinate himself.

Not what a planner likes to hear, of course. Understandably so, if you consider that he is usually somewhat more intelligent and better educated than his creative counterpart. Perhaps he can console himself in knowing that in Formula One racing the super-brain engineer has to work for a half-crazy driver who carries the largest part of his brain in his butt.

At Jung von Matt, we have no Strategic Planners. But we do have Efficiency Planners. Why did we interpret the role of planners differently? We took a look at the market and got the impression that, especially in Germany, there were mostly Placebo Planners.

By that we mean the many eloquent, charismatic advertisers who snow their clients into believing they have spent their time well rather than specifically invigorating the creative process. Planners who are more "New Business Weapons" than efficiency experts. Planners who want to turn advertising into something that will, in time, cut off its own air supply: a science.

A lack of space can release energy, a lack of air can't.

THOSE WHO WANT TO TAKE THE CONSUMER'S BREATH AWAY MUST GIVE THE CREATIVE PEOPLE PLENTY OF AIR TO BREATHE.

We don't want the planner to simply give us the best approach for landing a deal with a customer. We also want him to blanket the runway with inspiration. To find unusual ways to present the knowledge and wishes of our clients.

Once, when we were advertising a children's product, we were faced with the problem that very few of our creative people had any points of reference dealing with 8- to 12-year-olds. And all the empirical research we could find was frozen in theory. So our planner had school kids write compositions about advertising. The kids were pleased with the old Apple computer we gave them in return. And the creative team got experience that conventional market research couldn't provide.

For instance, Maya, 10, wrote: "Without advertising, TV would be a big mess. One film would follow another one right away." And: "I like Ricola. When the man sings, it sounds so funny that I laugh really hard and I totally miss the rest of the spot." Good to know.

Another unusual method helped us to convince a client that the decision to buy his product didn't involve just men and women, but that the kids also had something to say. Or at least they had some kind of veto. Our planners went into schoolyards and filmed teenagers talking about the advertised product.

Irreverent sentences were uttered. With terms like "embarrassing" and "lame." We had rarely seen a board of directors so fascinated by a TV screen.

It is crucial that strategic planning doesn't end with campaign development but accompanies each account throughout the process. With regular client contact, with "brand days," and, most of all, with constant efficiency control. Because we believe that you can't blindly follow the same track—nice and easy, the way it used to be—but that you have to adjust to exponentially growing trend dynamics.

According to the motto, "In a changing environment, only those who are constantly adapting can stay the same." And this means adapting with a goal. That's why, at Jung von Matt, we gave the planners a different title and responsibilities.

We expect them to focus on the problem, for example. The efficiency planner should focus on the problem 100%, so that the creative guy can focus on the solution 100%. Fewer overlaps mean better results. You know what too many cooks do to a broth.

The planner is therefore responsible for inspiring the creative people. Not for regulating. And absolutely not for dictating.

As we mentioned before, more than ever, advertising has to be as right as necessary and as fascinating as possible. The compulsory program must be sufficient, the free-style event must be thrilling. Many agencies try, however, to elevate the compulsory component, i.e., correctness. They use checklists and choose the solution that gets the most ticks.

The second service we expect from an efficiency planner is focussed disenchantment. It may be public knowledge that we advertisers tend to think that we are more important than we really are. Just because our films are shown more often on TV than those of Steven Spielberg, just because our posters are bigger than Paul Cezanne's "The Bay From l'Estaque" we think we are

THE MASTERS OF THE UNIVERSE.

Roman generals must have had a similar problem. Because every one of them had a slave travel with him on his triumphant processions whose sole task was to gripe and curse at the general so he wouldn't become a megalomaniac.

The planner is supposed to guide the creative team back to reality and sales figures. He is supposed to remind them that the point is not to make the ad agency famous but to make the brand desirable. And that their triumphs are measured by quantitative figures after all. We are convinced that this "contact with the ground crew" never did a good creative mind any harm.

That's why we also introduced the effectiveness planner's Report From the Front. It has only two categories — "cool" and "lame" — and describes, at the beginning of the month, any new information about the effectiveness of our campaigns.

PORSCHE "FAMILY CAR," PRINT 1992:
HEADLINE: "YOU CAN TAKE MORE TIME FOR BREAKFAST. YOU'RE BACK HOME EARLIER FOR DINNER. COULD THERE BE A BETTER FAMILY CAR?"
BECAUSE IT DEFIED THE USUAL, THIS CAMPAIGN WAS POLARIZING FROM DAY ONE. THE BOLD COLORS. THE BLURRY PICTURES. AND LAST BUT NOT LEAST THE HEADLINES. OF COURSE IT WAS TONGUE-IN-CHEEK TO PRESENT THE PORSCHE 911 AS A FAMILY CAR. BUT MANY TOOK IT SERIOUSLY AND NURTURED OUR THESIS—IRONY IS PURE LUCK.
THE NEXT HEADLINE READ: "FOR MORE THAN 100 YEARS CARS HAVE PROVIDED INDEPENDENCE. ONE WON'T."

PHOTOGRAPHER: UWE DÜTTMANN

THE BEST STRATEGISTS ARE LAZY GENIUSES

Other agencies might have self-critical efficiency reports about their own campaigns too. But we present these reports on the first of each month to everyone. As a regular reminder of what our job is all about in the end. Measurable results.

The third service we expect from planners is the "deadly pass." (In ice hockey, the pass that helps to score a goal is called an "assist," which supports our theory that the planner must work for the creative player.)

Successful assists—whether in sports or communications—have three characteristics. First, the pass must come as a total surprise. The most brilliant advertising is often simply a surprising strategy transformed with little creative meddling. Second, the pass must be played into a free zone. The planner must give the creative team room to act, perhaps provide them with some alternatives. Often a briefing provides more leeway for creativity than a limiting key phrase. And third, the pass must be easy to control. Planning doesn't just provide opportunities, it has risks as well. One example is the I-want-facts-facts-facts risk.

Why do companies with successful brands rarely do their own advertising? Because they know too much about their product and can no longer maintain objectivity. That's why it is absurd for us to pile up all kinds of knowledge. Too much insider knowledge hinders the creative team and is not productive for the planner. We believe in overview and visual judgment. And WE BELIEVE IN PARALYSIS BY ANALYSIS.

Speaking of knowledge. How educated do you have to be to create good advertising? Or, in other words, how knowledgeable should you be about your subject? That depends. Of course you have to know what an IT specialist wants to best advertise a mainframe computer. But you don't need a college education to advertise ice-cream — it might even get in the way of "Go Nogger yourself." Over the years, we have encountered many colleagues who exemplify the following principle:

SMART SMARTER OUTSMARTED.

The fact that planners are usually the best-educated employees in an ad agency tempts them to add creative accents. The I-can-be-creative-too risk.

Von Matt's first job in advertising was in the trafficking department. He was dedicated and couldn't bear that he had no creative influence whatsoever on the artwork masters he carried around all day. That's why he carved a tiny scratch into each master. And felt a mischievous glee when he later saw the ad in the paper with that tiny blemish.

Unfortunately, planners often have the same urge. Instead of stimulating and providing free creative space they start to develop concrete ideas and lose the necessary objectivity toward the creative product. The educated strategist is a sub-optimal creative person—just like the educated creative person is a sub-optimal strategist.

And finally, we would like to warn about the I-am-worth-my-salary risk. In our experience, in many cases the right strategy is obvious. The client knows what his brand needs. And the creative guy understands it right away. In these cases it is the strategist's job to do what is hardest for him — hold back. His assist is not needed.

Often, a planner putters around in a briefing simply to underscore his importance and justify his salary. This is how bad motives cause kinks in a straight line or create one loop too many in the thought process.

Once, we won an account because we followed the client's briefing blindly. We didn't have the time or the people for a critical analysis of the matter. Other agencies did, and arrived at completely different strategy recommendations. They went through a huge amount of trouble. And turned out to be the fools in the end.

The task was to present DEA as the most customer-friendly gas station network in Germany. One of our competitors ran a poll that reported that drivers don't care at all about friendly service, but rather about the fuel quality. Then they banked on a campaign that missed DEA's core clientele and the client's expectations by miles.

Any reservations we have when it comes to planners lie in false ambition and overzealousness. As elsewhere, "A lot will bring a lot" is the wrong mantra. Good planning is a mixture of ingenuity and laziness. Because too many facts drive the planner crazy. Too many planners drive the creative team crazy. And in clear cases like DEA, the planner should relax and step back.

Of course, even the ideal planner can't always help. Because his "right" research can't always be transformed into fascinating communication. Especially because he deducts rational theses based on his analysis, whereas fascinating advertising is often based on the irrational.

For Audi, we consistently came up with good advertising for "quattro" four-wheel drive. Audi's marketing people were keen on our not positioning the quattro models as "snowplows." Simply because the relevance of a snow-ready engine — for those few snowy days we have in Germany — hits only a very small target group.

Our planners went to work and came back with "The On-Road Four-Wheeler." So, the first four-wheeler was not meant to go off-road but, on the contrary, to stay on the road. We developed a TV commercial that corresponded exactly to this idea. The text, "Others build four-wheelers so they can go off-road. We build four-wheelers so you can stay on the road." The spot was right, but it was hardly fascinating.

At the same time, the American Audi agency developed a spot that was the perfect counterpart: fascinating, but hardly right. It showed an Eskimo father and son discovering animal tracks in the snow, and it delighted all of Germany. Who cared about the snowplow problem? We followed the briefing doggedly and drew the shorter straw. The clear runner-up. Beaten by two Eskimos. Their advertising experiment left our tried and true concept looking like crap. Why don't we get this kind of wake-up call more often?

Every productive enterprise engages in research and development. Because it wants to be better and more successful. Every car manufacturer invests money to develop new ideas and test new market possibilities. Pharmaceutical companies even more so. But also every soft-drink maker, commercial bakery, insurer, etc.

Why does this way of thinking not exist in the increasingly important communications industry? Why is there no research and development budget set aside for trying out new things? If ten percent of an ad account were invested in

R & D,

advertising would be more efficient by tomorrow. There would be a little less fuel to burn for the campaign but there would be many more chances to discover new sources of fascination.

The experience of creating a campaign with high momentum can mean a new relationship with communication. Just like a cheating wife who suddenly realizes what love can mean. Many enterprises live happily with their communications "same-old same-old." They simply don't know anything else. Then one day—ZOOM!

CHAPTER 8

THE BRAND'S JOURNEY FROM THE FLAG TO THE DRESS
ABOUT IMAGES, IDENTITY, AND IDENTIFICATION

What did the NSU RO 80 gain from the fact that it anticipated carmakers' design trends 20 years ahead of time? The respect of some experts, perhaps, but hardly market success. What did an Internet pioneer gain from the fact that, by the end of the 1980s, he had answers to questions nobody was asking yet? What does an avant-garde fashion designer gain by creating a new style that the big brands turn into big money a season later?

Marketing always preaches the importance of gaining the "First Mover Advantage" by being the first on the market. A prime example, Lindbergh, who was the first to cross the Atlantic in a nonstop flight, became famous. Chamberlin and Levine, who were second to do so, are complete unknowns. So are Köhl, Fitzmaurice, and von Hünefeld, who first crossed the Atlantic from east to west and so accomplished what fellow aviators consider the greater feat.

Of course, there are industries where only the one who is the first to offer his product can demand "first-of-the-season" prices.

Still, the first mover advantage formula must be questioned. He who comes late might be punished by life.

But: HE WHO COMES EARLY GETS PUNISHED BY THE MARKET.

The reality of economics shows that being consistent is often more important than being first.

Harvey R. Ball, who died on 12 April 2001 in his hometown of Worcester, Massachusetts, must have felt the same. The name won't mean much to you, and that was exactly Ball's biggest problem. Because like everyone else in the world you know his most famous product. And most certainly you like this product unless it has been spray painted on the wall of your house.

Harvey R. Ball is the inventor of the yellow smiley face, grinning at us from buttons, coffee mugs, underwear, and T-shirts, from traffic signs and house walls. Two dots and a line that make even a gravestone look happy.

THREE-SECOND MOMENTUM.

There is no other symbol that can create more positive emotion with less effort.

The story of the funny face wasn't funny for Ball because he forgot to register his Smiley as a trademark. Which meant that Smiley could make a lot of money. But not for Ball, who remained poor.

THE BRAND'S JOURNEY FROM THE FLAG TO THE DRESS

The Frenchman Franklin Loufrani recognized its true market value. In 1971, he registered the Smiley as a trademark in the US and in 79 other countries — claiming that he invented it, of course — and became filthy rich. If you use the symbol :) in an e-mail or an SMS message anytime soon, please remember the real inventor!

As this example shows, investing in a brand can have immeasurable value. A brand is, first and foremost, a thing. However, we do talk about its personality, its identity, its core. Brands are attributed with almost magical powers. Reason enough to celebrate the brand as an event. That's what makes it so valuable for consumers and trademark holders. So what's the difference between a product and a brand?

While a product is mainly functional, a brand also defines its owner. Of course there are differences for different types of products. A car brand defines its owner more than a corkscrew does. Although… it always depends on the personal interests and environment of each individual. The driver of a Mercedes-Benz doesn't just show that technical perfection matters to him, he also shows that sportiness and aesthetics are more important to him than superficial appeal of dynamics.

But let's get back to the corkscrew. You can get one for free in any drugstore. Can corkscrews become branded products? A wine connoisseur will barely raise an eyebrow. For him, there is a huge difference between a common corkscrew and the classic Château Laguiole when he approaches a 96 Margaux. A huge difference in price as well — the one costs less than

MERCEDES-BENZ "SLS," INTEGRATED CAMPAIGN 2009:
THE SLS WAS BUILT BY AMG AND IT WAS SUPPOSED TO BRING THE LEGEND OF THE SUPER SPORTS CAR 300 SL OF 1955 INTO THE FUTURE. AND WE WERE SUPPOSED TO DISSEMINATE THIS LEGEND WITH A RICH INTERACTIVE WEB SPECIAL AND HAVE IT FURTHER DISSEMINATED BY OVER A MILLION VISITORS.

DIRECTOR: BERND & JEFF
PRODUCTION: BM8

SIXT RENT A CAR "ANGELA MERKEL," PRINT 2001:
HEADLINE: "CARE FOR A NEW HAIRDO? JUST RENT A CONVERTIBLE."
PROBABLY THE MOST EFFICIENT AD IN THE HISTORY OF OUR AGENCY. IT WAS ONLY PRINTED ONCE, IN THE DAILY NEWSPAPER SÜDDEUTSCHE ZEITUNG AND IN THE WEEKLY MAGAZINE FOCUS. TOTAL COST: 95,000 EUROS. BU WHEN ALL TV FEATURES AND REPORTS ABOUT THIS AD ARE ADDED IN, THE RESULTING MEDIA VALUE AMOUNTS TO 3.2 MILLION EUROS. AND BEST OF ALL:
MS. MERKEL PROVED SHE HAD A GREAT SENSE OF HUMOR.

PHOTOGRAPHER: ACTION PRESS & ANDRÉ MÜHLING

2.50 euros, the other about 100 euros. Both work. But only one of them has momentum — provided that you have an audience who can decode this product's iconicity.

In "No Logo," the journalist and globalization critic Naomi Klein gives a detailed description of how this shift from the production of merchandise to the production of image came to be, and what the consequences are. Nike, for example, one of the leading companies in this process, has an advertising budget that, by 1997, had become twenty times bigger than it was in 1987.

Nike doesn't advertise a specific athletic shoe. Nike advertises Nike. Marketing is no longer about single products but about the company's image.

NIKE DOESN'T SELL SHOES.
NIKE SELLS DREAMS, PERSPECTIVES, THOUGHTS.

The 20 million dollars Nike paid basketball great Michael Jordan in 1992 was more than they paid the entire Indonesian work force of 30,000 people who produced the shoes. It becomes increasingly clear that it isn't only the media who produce culture on a global scale, rather, all industrial sectors participate in the production of culture.

Microsoft, Apple, Nike, Swatch, Coca-Cola, Calvin Klein, Benetton, McDonald's, and Body Shop have become as influential as the classic producers of culture such as Time Warner and Walt Disney. Even if advertisers can't really take credit for it: the Body Shop brand did it without classic advertising.

Brands and their symbolic content shed their geographical boundaries long ago. A Nike shoe is as well known in the USA as it is in Scandinavia or Southeast Asia. But it is also important that people everywhere know what it means to own a Nike shoe. Global presence by uniform brand presentation—assisted by the new media, which has radically simplified the worldwide handling of brand presentation.

But one issue seems important in this context, since it has far-reaching consequences for client and customer alike. If you follow Jeremy Rifkin, economics journalist and president of the think tank "Foundation on Economic Trends" in Washington, the present economy is transforming itself into a network connecting enterprise, supplier, and customer (Rifkin, 2000).

We are on the way from market to network. From property to access,

FROM OWNER TO USER.

A car manufacturer will soon no longer sell cars, but will charge a fee for the period of time a car is used. The consumer will always get the latest model delivered to his front door. Contact with the brand will not happen just once, during the sale, but throughout the use of the car. The brand will accompany the customer and have countless opportunities to communicate with him and give him access to other offers.

In the automobile sector, innovative utilization concepts are becoming more and more realistic. With his project "Better Place,"

Israel-born Shai Agassi is planning a revolutionary system, which solves both the recharging time problem as well as the reach limitations of electromobility: for a monthly service fee, a country-wide network of e-charging stations will provide a fully automated battery exchange, which does not take any longer than filling a conventional tank with 12 gallons of gasoline.

Let's imagine consumer relationships as a form of cultural representation. By immersing himself into these mixed worlds of product and experience, the user proves to the world that he belongs to a certain way of life, a certain social stratum. As Rifkin put it, "Without culture, commerce cannot exist."

The influential French sociologist Pierre Bourdieu tied social recognition to the acquisition of signs of symbolic wealth (Bourdieu, 1982). These are symbolic characteristics that have the effect of differentiating. They contribute to one person being different from another. They illuminate social differences and tiers.

Social recognition comes from the possession not of economic capital — material money and wealth — but of symbolic capital. Those who have more symbolic capital have a stronger social presence, their existence and singularity is recognized. Thus, discernable symbols represent the all-or-nothing boundary between the haves and have-nots.

In that sense, all things and practices have intrinsic differentiating characteristics. They draw their respective value, their basic social meaning from their relative position in the total system of discernible symbols. A few years ago, the cell phone had such a function. Now, Germany has more mobile phones than normal phones.

A TV commercial for cheap cell phone rates showed a manager in his limousine at a stoplight, where a young kid was washing the car windows. Suddenly a cell phone rings. The manager starts to look for it. But it is the boy who reaches into his pocket. Today, you would ask yourself "So, where's the punch line?" Thirteen years ago, this was a surprising script. The product has long since lost its ability to define its owner.

It is interesting that the difference between economic and symbolic capital seems to be valid for companies as well. Let's look again at Nike. The number one company in the sports world doesn't own production sites. Nike owns—frankly—nothing but a name and licenses. Symbolic capital in the form of a brand idea and a brand name. Adidas-Salomon also has a manufacturing depth of only 4%.

McDonald's realized very early on that selling an idea was more lucrative than selling hamburgers. Most of the branches do not belong to McDonald's but to partners who lease the franchise rights from McDonald's for a limited time. Most important are the brand idea and the brand name. And the chance to give the customer access to the brand's world of experience.

This has far-reaching consequences for the launch of a brand, since the parameters for communication have changed completely. Cultural meaning cannot be represented by functional

THE BRAND'S JOURNEY FROM THE FLAG TO THE DRESS

value alone. And if it is, it soon becomes apparent that the rationale behind the functional value of different products becomes interchangeable.

It's no secret. We live in an era of competitive markets. There is a huge selection of anything and everything. When a new product enters the market, the competition hits almost immediately. Just think about the first handheld digital camcorder—first JVC, then Sony. Or the organic yogurt LC1—you'd have to be practically bionic to stand out in the dairy cooler now. You might also want to provide a copy of Kant's "Critique of Judgment" near each cooler. In technology or on grocery shelves, there is a constant race between products. Rational arguments are increasingly relegated to the background.

There are too many things, there is simply too much uninteresting, interchangeable stuff. Everywhere you look! And if rationality becomes too complex, the human mind switches to emotionality. This phenomenon is particularly obvious in political advertising. When the voter loses sight of the issues in the swirl of election programs, he orients himself by looking at faces. And votes for the one that seems most trustworthy.

The consequence: in communications, you invest in feelings. You build emotional worlds for successful brands and thus create an emotional added value that elevates a brand above all the other versions of the same product, and differentiates it from the competition. And we practically drown in a flood of clichés.

BABY + DOG = FAMILY BLISS,

laughing woman + flower bouquet = female bliss, jewelry + heart = love, white-haired gentleman gone fishing or with grandchild = carefree old age, young people with old American convertible = youthful offer, gray-haired couple on Harley-Davidson = vitality in old age, man doing kitchen chores = self-confident woman. Loosely based on the philosophy "Show what you will get."

Admittedly, this compartmentalized way of thinking helps sort out and organize the tide of information and impulses constantly pounding us all.

But cliché images that follow the equation "Show a consumer in a happy situation and everybody will instantly recognize that his well-being can be clearly traced back to the product in question" cannot be expected to generate high momentum. The formula "Show certain feelings = Create certain feelings" is simply too simple. Will a middle-aged woman in a cut-off sweater imitating Britney Spears turn into a new Lolita? Will a dignified older gentleman who conducts his banking online become a post-modern trendsetter?

Nevertheless, a simple formula outweighs all others. Because it allows for a simple, direct evaluation of communication. As a client, you feel understood. And you have a good grip on the final result. It is pleasant to tread on the solid ground of linear structures. But the consumer never feels the way he

BALLANTINE'S "WOMAN ON THE BEACH," PRINT 2001:
HEADLINE: "PEELS, SPLIT ENDS, STINGS, TOO BIG, JUST FINE" BALLANTINE'S GERMAN IMPORTER MANAGED TO HIRE US OVER THE COMPANY'S PREFERRED INTERNATIONAL AGENCY. BUT UNFORTUNATELY JUST FOR ONE YEAR, THEN THE MANUFACTURER PUT HIS FOOT DOWN. THAT SAME YEAR WE LOST ANOTHER WORLDWIDE BRAND TO AN INTERNATIONAL NETWORK, ALTHOUGH THE GERMAN IMPORT COMPANY FOUGHT FOR US. IT WAS MICROSOFT.

PHOTOGRAPHER: MICHAEL SCHNABEL

is supposed to. He feels the way he wants to. To make him want to feel the way he is supposed to, we have to surprise and trick him. Communication is like a fishpond. The bait has to be appealing to the target group, not to the person with the rod.

YOU USED TO LISTEN TO WHAT A BRAND HAD TO SAY.
NOW YOU HAVE TO SIT DOWN AND COMMUNICATE WITH IT.

Even more importantly, the brand communicates for you. It expresses a way of life, an identity. Another reason why a brand's behavior is often more important than its message. When you listen to a speech, you are listening for an opinion. When you go and have a beer with the speaker afterwards, you want more. And these days, you and your trusted brand go and have a beer.

The meaning of communication has exploded because the concept of "brand" has changed—from flag to dress. Brands used to point the way, help with orientation in the supply jungle. Today, they are part of your personality.

FORGET ABOUT **CLOTHES MAKE THE MAN**.
NOW IT'S **BRANDS MAKE THE MAN**.

When brands become carriers of meaning, they offer an infinite potential for differentiation, because communication has a huge supply of signs at its disposal.

Just like in motor racing, differentiation doesn't work on the ideal line. Those who want to pass others, who want to attack, must get off this line. Maybe pick a layout that breaks with the usual sensibilities. Many advertisers forget about this. They are talked onto the ideal line by market research and end up with completely interchangeable and thus inefficient campaigns.

Our job is differentiation. Differentiation is the opposite of conformity. In practice, this means that all concepts have to be turned into Unique Selling Propositions. The essential value of a product is not its functional use value but its potential to confer status. The product can thus become a kind of iconic symbolism, a language read and understood by the user. A brand is positioned by the added value of emotions.

But doesn't differentiating a brand by using emotional added value expose it to the risk of having to change its message radically — and expensively — every time the meaning of a sign changes? In its lifetime, every brand has many chances to win attention and interest. These chances often pop up unexpectedly, at an event, by a serendipitous acquaintance, through cooperation.

Unfortunately, these chances don't always fall exactly on a brand's strategic track. It's a shame if they aren't exploited simply because they don't follow the plan. Particularly since flexibility and presence of mind are characteristics that can give additional depth to any brand. Those who lack the

COURAGE TO FACE DISCONTINUITY

lose efficiency. They fear losing their way. Consistency and stamina are always—and rightfully so—seen as efficiency boosters. The only way to make a 3 million euro budget into a 30 million euro budget is to let the 3 million campaign run unchanged for ten years. And not completely change campaigns every couple of years, which seems to be every brand's fate these days. Only 15% of the large brands have maintained continuity over the past ten years.

Changes in advertising budgets are closely tied to future earnings. American scientists have proven in a long-term study that, depending on the sector, advertising activities are significantly tied to earnings for up to four years (Graham/Frankenberger, 2000). The earnings contribution is highest during the first year and steadily decreases over the next few years. This means that advertising budgets are a long-term reservoir for momentum. Advertisers should remember this when they cut their budgets in economically taxing times. They deprive themselves of a good starting position in the subsequent boom period.

Continuity in a collaboration with an ad agency is also apparent in the client's stock market value. A ten-year study proved that the reassessment or termination of an agency relationship lead to a significant decrease in the company's stock price (Hozier/Schatzberg, 2000). Obviously, investors react to those signals and reduce their expectations concerning stock market development and dividend payment.

Another decisive advantage of continuity is that it provides a basis for flexibility. Those who steer a steady course are better positioned to take occasional detours than those whose brands start out on shaky ground.

Driving provides another good example for this. The best way to avoid obstacles is stay on a dynamically neutral course. That's why a racecar driver briefly hits the brakes after a curve to steer better into the next one. More simply said:

HAVE YOU EVER SEEN A GOALKEEPER STANDING ON ONE LEG DURING A PENALTY KICK?

The Sixt brand demonstrates true continuity in communication. And that's why this brand can risk the occasional ricochet beyond strategy lines. For example, "Better too Sixt than too expensive." A slogan that didn't correspond to the strategy "Drive business class, pay economy," but was used simply because of its creative quality.

During the total eclipse in the summer of 1999, the agency came up with the idea "Due to the total eclipse, convertibles are half off." When the topic of Leitkultur, or "leading culture" was discussed in all the media, we came up with "Sixt on Leitkultur," advertising cars with navigational systems. And when there were rumors that Mercedes was planning to buy Sixt we countered with "The rumor: Mercedes bought Sixt. The truth: Sixt bought Mercedes—1,000 new C-Class models."

But not only Sixt displays presence of mind. When everyone was talking about Viagra, Mey fine Bodywear placed an ad that juxtaposed a pill and an erotic piece of lingerie. "Different agent, same effect."

By the way, Viagra itself is one of the best examples of how lucrative it can be to stray from a planned course. Its active ingredient, sildenafil, was originally intended to treat angina pectoris.

As usual, voluntary tests were conducted before introduction into the market, where patients were to try out the drug and return the remainder. But something unexpected happened: the patients didn't return anything. They discovered a wonderful side effect. And the Pfizer company was flexible enough to throw all their planning overboard. Thus one of the most successful drugs of all time was created.

Very few companies are flexible and fast enough to jump on the opportunity wagon and claim the

"VIAGRA EFFECT."

Many times we have tried to take advantage of opportunities like these. And we kept hearing from the marketing executives, "We didn't plan for that in the budget." "This doesn't match our current strategy." What they really meant to say was, "I don't have the guts to run with an action that wasn't approved by the board."

Few companies are consistent in presenting their brand profiles. They differ from others who throw themselves wholeheartedly into a campaign for a couple of years and then radically change course. Instead, they see their campaign as a flexible organism, provided it has the right genes.

They update the campaign here and there and re-evaluate its differentiating qualities in light of current trends. These brands see their consumers as partners who deserve more than to be bored by the same old stuff, to whom they can show some astonishing sides of the product without losing their unique character. A brand with long-lasting success looks at continuity not as status quo but as the basis for agility.

CHAPTER 9

IF YOU WANT TO LEAD BRANDS TO SUCCESS, YOU HAVE TO BE A SUCCESS YOURSELF
ABOUT MARKETING AN AD AGENCY

Ad agencies can do what nobody else can—they turn a product with functional use value into a brand with emotional added value. In short, they make brands. So they like to talk about brand building and brand leadership. But if you take a look at their own brand, all you find is neglected housework. Two out of three ad agencies violate two out of three brand rules.

Agency brands typically have a more or less timeless logo. Most often red. There's letterhead, envelopes and labels for packages, maybe DVDs. And there are business cards and greeting cards. That's it. Is that enough for a brand whose most important task is brand leadership?

Our point of view has always been that agency brands are subject to the same requirements and parameters for success as any other brand. The harmonic chord of branding can be applied to us as well: the perfect harmony of being well-known, well-liked, and useful.

If a client doesn't know anything about his brand, we ad people are outraged and prescribe market research. But what do we know! We often don't have a clue about what our own team thinks about our agency. Pretty sad if employees see their company differently than the managers do. And if management doesn't recognize the need for action because the erosion indicators haven't reached the top floor.

The American advertiser Jerry Della Femina once noted somberly that the first one to know about a budget loss is the doorman. It's like adultery. When the cuckold finally finds out, the whole block already knows.

The best early warning system for an agency brand's loss of attractiveness is a sinking number of applications for creative jobs. Often, the slow demise of a top agency has gone like this — no funny little colorful letters today, no serious paying customers tomorrow.

What makes our job unusual is that we are court jester and trustee rolled into one. On the one hand, we represent a light, even shallow, side. On the other hand, it's all about a lot of money.

ADVERTISING IS TOO EXPENSIVE TO FOOL AROUND WITH IT.

The client expects us to make his brand successful. He assumes that we know exactly what making a brand successful entails. The tricky part is that he only believes us if we are successful as well. An ad agency with sporadic flops is no longer believable as a "success wizard." And that's heading down a dangerous spiral. For that reason, ad agency brands are particularly sensitive. And as an active agency member you have to do even more to take care of your brand.

Of course, flops are part of the advertising business. Not every campaign has the desired effect, not every client stays for ten years, not every employee gets it. As a result, a TV commercial or a print ad gets panned by the press every now and then. Or there is speculation about the impending loss of an account. In cases like this, the same thing always happens. One of us gets terribly upset until the other reminds him that we owe the press for our success as well. None other than the press made us one of the best-known ad agencies in Germany. Through countless articles and interviews in almost all the economic and trade magazines, as well as visits on TV talk shows like Biolek or with Harald Schmidt, Germany's own David Letterman. The press even facilitated a casual afternoon chat with German Chancellor, Gerhard Schröder.

Just like any other brand, agency brands must make sure they are sufficiently visible to their target group. They have to provide guarantees about the quality of their products, which means the quality of their campaigns. And they must offer an emotional added value that elevates the agency brand beyond its fundamental purpose of creating good advertising.

Jung von Matt was not created from a theoretical insight that it was time for a new kind of agency. An agency that would make its mark as a brand more consistently than all the agencies up to that time. Jung von Matt was created because Jung and von Matt came to know and appreciate each other at the right time in their lives. Because both were open-minded enough and living a lifestyle that made it possible to embark on a bold and daring new career. Rent under 800 euros (utilities included), motorcycle all paid for, no mortgage, no family, no alimony or child support.

Good horses come from good stables, and we came from one of the best—Springer & Jacoby, who are still setting the standard to this day. We witnessed this Wunderkind agency's swift ascent to the Champions League, and we were inspired. We wanted something of our own, and that was more important than "my house, my car, my boat."

But what if we couldn't make it? If we couldn't keep a customer or, worst of all, produce any outstanding creative campaigns? The other agencies were also intensely interested in our launch. From concerned support: "If you need money, give me a call." To affectionate teasing: "Why don't you call yourself

jungfrAu und mAtterhorn."

At the beginning of the 1990s, the economy wasn't in an exactly euphoric state. But we believed that a recession was the ideal time to start an ad agency. Clients are restless and advertising budgets aren't tied down. Our launch happened to coincide with a wave of bankruptcies among other small agencies. The unlucky owners thought the increasing internationalization of business was to blame. And we became insecure. Does an independent agency stand a chance in an era of globalization? Are we doomed to rely on a network for support, or work only for furniture stores and tanning salons?

But we noticed that globalization wasn't quite what it was supposed to be. Just think of the following example. The most successful product in modern communications technology is called HANDY in Germany, MOBILE PHONE in England, PORTABLE in France, CELLULAR in America, TELEFONINO in Italy and NATEL in Switzerland. We know that it is possible to nurture worldwide brands independent of networks. And that globalization, when it finally arrives, can close as many doors as it can push open.

Another encouraging factor was the scarcity of creative talent. Bayern München's star player Mehmet Scholl once pleaded: "I'll waive my 50,000 euro salary if you just let me play." An independent agency benefits from exactly this trend. Because here's where creative players can play. Their talent is needed and put to good use, their work printed and broadcast.

Of course, we have to pay good salaries. But not compensation for inflicted pain, like many network agencies who mainly adapt ads for different markets and manage global campaigns. For a thoroughbred advertiser, it is as fulfilling to adapt a French TV commercial for German TV as it is for a thoroughbred soccer player to drag a net full of soccer balls to the training field.

Agencies who specialize in adapting advertising are hardly attractive for creative people, and will have a hard time finding

CONCERT HALL DORTMUND "CONCERT MILK," INTEGRATED ADVERTISING IDEA 2010: COWS GIVE MORE MILK WHEN THEY HEAR PRETTY MUSIC — IT IS SCIENTIFIC FACT. THEREFORE, THE MUSICIANS OF THE CONCERT HALL DORTMUND GAVE AN EXCLUSIVE CONCERT FOR 180 COWS. AND WE INTRODUCED THE MILK TO GROCERY STORES AS "CONCERT MILK." AN IDEA THAT WAS WELL RECEIVED FAR BEYOND DORTMUND.

DIRECTOR: SILVIO HELBIG

them. That's why they don't create many exceptional campaigns. And that's why there are not many clients who believe in the special momentum of such campaigns. The Captain from Köpenick syndrome of the advertising business—no job without an apartment, no apartment without a job.

Another effect was also advantageous for us. At the beginning of the 1990s, private TV stations really got off the ground. Finally, smaller advertisers had a chance to create TV commercials. Many took that chance, even if they were intimidated by the medium, and sought out competent guidance through the unknown territory of advertising films. No wonder, productions can cost up to 1 million euros.

The paper Super was an ambitious attempt by Hubert Burda and Rupert Murdoch to conquer the new German states with a tabloid newspaper. And we were their agency. Our creative people drove through East Germany in a camper asking a wide variety of people what they wanted in a newspaper and filming the answers. Many of the citizens we interviewed in the new German states declined their reimbursement for the following reason:

"I JUST GAVE MY HONEST OPINION.
AND I DON'T WANT MONEY FOR THAT."

From this video documentation, we created our first really unusual TV campaign. And a piece of history.

Soon we experienced our own meteoric rise, like the one we witnessed at Springer & Jacoby, and the brash newcomer Jung von Matt became a respected agency that the competition took seriously. The sudden growth surprised us but didn't make us insecure. Most of all, it forced us to come up with ideas to make our company leaner and faster. We tried to utilize our creative potential for higher work efficiency.

To escape the danger of long meetings, we came up with conference tables at which you had to stand—as high as a counter in a bar. And surprise! No more long meetings. And if meetings did stretch on, they were endured courageously. Von Matt has always had his best ideas in the car, in the shower, or on the toilet. To simulate this situation we invented the thinking cell—a small closet with a computer hook-up, to be a getaway for anyone who needed it. Maybe there is something to be said for von Matt's kinship with Nikolaus von Flüe, the patron saint of Switzerland, who left his wife and ten children to be able to write in peace and quiet.

All good ideas for the company, but none of them was meant to create a brand out of Jung von Matt. Then another idea came to the rescue. It was simple fate that our earliest clients came from the south of Germany. On our flights from Hamburg, we were among our number one target group, business travelers. Decision-makers and managers. Those who decide which agency to use or who are at least part of the decision-making process. We always carried a portable video recorder to be able to play back our first TV commercials. Our travel agency never understood why we always booked middle seats on every flight.

We also made a medium out of our portfolios by having them made in our house color, dark green, and having our logo prominently displayed on the front and back. No one had done it before and it triggered curiosity.

The Trojan horse was added later. As we mentioned earlier, the image came up during a presentation and has since been used again and again. Most of the listeners could understand this three-dimensional comparison. So we started to cultivate the whole thing and built a large Trojan horse for our reception area. In the fall of 2001, the four meter high wooden sculpture was brought to the historical museum "Haus der Geschichte" in Bonn where it was part of the exhibition "Celebrities in Advertising." Of course, our horse was not supposed to be merely a symbol but also a representation of a dynamic culture. We asked all our employees to model their arguments on the Trojan horse — a potent message in a friendly package.

But why stop there. We wanted to find our own way as an agency, to evaluate things ourselves, and asked ourselves, "Is there any virtue that rarely exists in the business?" We found one — self-criticism! Never have we heard an agency executive exclaim after a lost pitch:

"WE WERE NOT GOOD ENOUGH."

It's always someone else's fault, never one's own. The decision was supposedly helped by a relationship, the marketing boss was bribed. Or the client simply had no clue about communication.

We wanted to revolutionize this industry standard. And thus

the following unwritten law came to be: When we lose, it is always our fault. Maybe our concept was weak. Maybe it was too cocky. Or we may have been too expensive. But we are always the ones to blame.

We immediately sent out a questionnaire to our clients, who could check off answers as to why we weren't convincing; as to why we did not win their business. And of course we extended our congratulations to the winner.

It is also taboo to obsess about whether we won after a presentation is over. Has the ad campaign executive called back yet? Did the chairman of the board give you a big smile when we left? Did you notice how concrete their comments became towards the end?

We went through the usual wishing and hoping after presentations in other agencies far too many times — it amounts to nothing and just drains energy. And energy is what you need for the next challenge. Our first partner, Deneke von Weltzien, hit it on the spot:

"FIRE AND FORGET."

Unlike most of our colleagues, we are not against competitive presentations, but for them. For the agency, they are the best way to win over a customer, and for the customer they are the safest way to pick an agency. It is partly striving for peak performance and partly looking for the truth.

JUNG VON MATT "THE MARRIAGE CANDIDATES," PRINT 2000:
HEADLINE: "EVERY OTHER MARRIAGE STARTS OUT AT THE WORKPLACE."
OF COURSE JUNG VON MATT BELIEVES IN SELF-ADVERTISING. WE RAN A LARGE FORMAT AD AT THE LAUNCH OF OUR AGENCY. THE AD WITH THE NAKED JVM EMPLOYEES ALSO HAD A GREAT EFFECT, TOO BAD IT WASN'T FOR US PERSONALLY. ONE YEAR LATER THREE OF OUR FOUR EMPLOYEES WERE LURED AWAY BY THE COMPETITION.

PHOTOGRAPHER: UWE DÜTTMANN

IF YOU WANT TO LEAD BRANDS TO SUCCESS, YOU HAVE TO BE A SUCCESS YOURSELF

Top achievements only come out of competitive situations. To test one's boundaries, and go beyond them, you need strong opponents against whom you absolutely do not want to lose. And a showdown that grabs everyone's attention. All that is possible only in a competitive situation.

And truth finding also goes against awarding a budget without a campaign presentation. It's a bit like getting married without having had sex. Because it is difficult to find out if the partnership between agency and client has a future. And if the latter really has the courage he claims.

In all aspects of the job, there is a big difference whether you find something in an agency by accident or whether you can use defined rules for certain processes. Rules are cultivated values based on experience. They serve a brand better than habit alone.

For example, it might be useful for an agency to conduct live street interviews with consumers in certain cases, and to show the client a short video presentation of the results. We made these videos a standard tool, and use them at every stage to steer the creative process.

Conventional market research fails in this regard because it is too slow. A "trend video" can tell us in a couple of hours if our slogan recommendation actually hits the mark. A trend video is to conventional market research what a pistol is to a rifle. It's not quite as accurate, but in the heat of battle it's the only thing that works. And we have never experienced a presentation without heat.

An essential element of our quality-oriented brand knowledge is our monthly Report from the Front. We are not satisfied with producing creative solutions; we want to know how the campaigns are working. As we have mentioned before, all Jung von Matt employees are informed regularly about whether we have reached campaign goals.

Rules and tools have to be internalized by all the people working for a brand. But ad agencies employ strong individualists, not Pavlov's dogs. That's why every instrument, every rule is constantly tested.

It is the same with creative ideas. If there is no convincing direction, the whole campaign lacks cohesion. It is basically sweated out.

Ignorance, on the other hand, has nothing to do with sweating. That's why brand managers are forced to recite their product features like parrots. And keep a tight rein on troublemakers who always try to change everything. Not because what they have isn't successful but simply because they get bored.

BRAND MANAGEMENT
HAS A LOT TO DO WITH STAMINA!

Looking at other sectors always leads to self-doubt. And there are always new ideas coming from the innermost circle of the company suggesting that you modify or even abolish all things traditional. Other brands' successes are always cited as examples that it's time to change tried and true behavior.

IF YOU WANT TO LEAD BRANDS TO SUCCESS, YOU HAVE TO BE A SUCCESS YOURSELF

An agency must live up to every demand they make on themselves, including on their own product, their ads. It isn't just about winning creative awards. It is about proving that we would walk through fire for our principles. That we would sometimes refuse lucrative business if the restrictions placed upon us endangered the quality of the advertising in the long run. Basically, think brand, not short-term gain. Just the way we advertisers always preach to our clients.

Even if advertising has nothing to do with art, there is a point of contact at this juncture. People only believe in the artist's conviction toward his artistic endeavor if he is willing to forsake all the amenities of a secure life as a normal citizen. Artistic breakthrough is often preceded by years of hunger and struggle.

The same holds for an agency brand. The general insecurity about evaluating creative achievement can be overcome if there is proof that the agency acts out of conviction. And if that reputation is already out there.

As a consequence, an agency must sometimes choose quality over business. Even if it goes against the standard in our industry that an agency stays true to its client until it gets replaced and finds it harder to land a job.

"MAN BITES DOG"

is just not believable. "Dog bites man" makes a lot more sense.

IF YOU WANT TO LEAD BRANDS TO SUCCESS, YOU HAVE TO BE A SUCCESS YOURSELF

It is only possible for a brand to grow on the slippery slope of communication services if luck, ambition, stubbornness, and flexibility combine at the right time and place with an overwhelming desire to achieve. An agency brand that has proven its knowledge of brand leadership by leading itself to success.

But what does the client get from an agency that has itself become a brand? In the end, it's what a housewife gets from her favorite detergent—guaranteed quality.

Only an agency with a deeper interest in the success of its campaigns can be a true partner. Only then can the client be assured of getting professional advice that is closely oriented to the campaign's success.

Only a partner who is proud of his achievements gives everything. An agency that has something to lose if it produces mediocrity stays objective with its clients.

It is no different than the usual employee or management participation models. "Caught together, hanged together" is the principle with the most potential to mobilize motivation and achievement. And precisely that motivating push can be guaranteed if an agency puts as much emphasis on its own interests as a brand as on those of its clients.

In an era where everyone wants to be a brand, it is wise to trust only those agencies that also see themselves as a brand. And that prove brand leadership where it can hurt most—behind its own doors! Spiegel magazine called us the "pop stars of advertising." If this means we are the harbingers of a particularly popular type of advertising, we are flattered.

"If Springer & Jacoby are the Beatles, then Jung von Matt are the Rolling Stones," wrote Manager Magazin. If this means we are like a band that has kept its passion alive for about 50 years and lost none of its momentum, we are doubly flattered.

CHAPTER 10

THE TRAINING WHEELS OF MARKETING
ABOUT THE QUESTIONABLE NATURE OF OPINION POLLS

If you happen to walk past our agency in Hamburg's Karolinenviertel in the St. Pauli district, please do so with you head high, your shoulders squared, and at a steady pace.

The criminologist's insight says that people who appear to be insecure are more likely to be victims of a crime than those who appear to be self-confident. There must be a difference — apparently subtle but irrefutable — between tentativeness and security. And precisely the same difference exists in economics.

A brand product manager conducting an opinion poll sends out the following signal: I'm not quite sure. And that spark of insecurity can ignite a wildfire of insecurity in the respondent.

Consider for a moment what goes through your mind when you get polled. If someone asks you for directions, for example, do you assume that person already knows the way? If someone asks you for permission, does he already know he will get it? If someone asks you about your opinion of his new car, can he be sure that you think it's great? Simply

ASKING SIGNALS WEAKNESS.

And that's a fundamental problem of market research.

When American opinion pollsters once asked: "Do you think that the individual wrongdoings of people—not the conditions of society—are responsible for the increase in crime," two thirds of the respondents said yes. But when they asked instead: "Do you think that the conditions in today's society—not the individual wrongdoings of people—are responsible for increasing crime," two thirds of the respondents also said yes. In order to avoid the pressure of explaining themselves, people prefer to answer yes rather than no in opinion polls.

As David Ogilvy wrote in his 1963 classic "Confessions of an Advertising Man," "...[marketing executives] are coming to rely too much on research, and they use it as a drunkard uses a lamp post for support, rather than for illumination."

Nevertheless, over the past 25 years, the revenue of market research institutes has increased disproportionately to the revenue of ad agencies. Obviously, there is a growing desire in our sector to ask for directions. Preferably during the first stages of realization, before the campaign is set in motion, and before a lot of effort and money are spent on production. Each institute has its specific test designs, experiences, and research techniques, but all promise the same thing—greater security in decisions concerning questions about communication.

EVERY ADVERTISER'S DREAM:
CAMPAIGNS WITHOUT RISK!

Reality is sobering. If it weren't, there wouldn't be as many flops. One can assume that all new product launches, all larger campaigns and especially all new campaign launches, have gone through more or less elaborate testing. However, the flop rate is exceptionally high. For grocery products it is nearly 85%; for certain types of merchandise as high as 98%. This means that investments for new launches, in the amount of about 18 billion euros per year, are recklessly and regularly frittered away (Becker, 1993). Momentum simply can't be anticipated by tests.

Neither can failure be anticipated by the fact that a campaign is radically rejected by a target group. What is important is that the radical rejectors are balanced by radical supporters. A theoretical example, two cigarette campaigns are tested. We are dealing with a product where communication is key. The brand has a market share of 5%. One campaign achieves 79% support, the other only 44%. Without hesitation, the cigarette manufacturer uses the 79% campaign.

Possibly a mistake. Who can tell us that the 1% market share gain that the campaign is supposed to produce can be found in the 79% group rather than in the 44% group? Isn't it more likely that the obviously polarizing campaign with 44% might trigger more momentum in that 1%? The brand product industry often has its mind set blindly on quantity. They want to increase market shares and they ask the majority to do it for them.

How unreasonable this focus on the majority can be is demonstrated by ultra-conservative Ronald Barnabas Schill's success in Hamburg's state elections. Even though his unmistakable message stirred up general resistance, he achieved a sensational 19% of the vote. Obviously, this result would never have been

WELT AM SONNTAG "KOHL," TV SPOT 2000:
THIS TV SPOT RAN AT THE HEIGHT OF THE PARTY
DONATION SCANDAL. THE IDEA WAS TO LET HELMUT
KOHL BE SILENT FOR A MINUTE. QUITE A CHALLENGE
FOR A MAN WHO SPENT HIS WHOLE LIFE SPEAKING
IN FRONT OF CAMERAS. AND OBVIOUSLY NOT A REAL
PLEASURE. AFTER THE THIRD TAKE HE SAID "GENTLE-
MEN, THAT'S IT!" AND LEFT.

possible if he had soft-boiled his campaign promise according to market research recommendations. Election projections placed him at around 13%, by the way.

Empirical proof for the power of polarization can be found in the Youngcom! Youth Study 2000. Those brands most often labeled as "brands with the best advertising" were also labeled as "brands with the worst advertising" by the same group of 13- to 20-year-olds.

Most important for efficient handling of market research is a reasonable goal. Curiosity and search for excellence beat out security and lack of decisiveness. It is all about getting more things right. And not about getting fewer things wrong. Sounds banal, but makes a big difference when dealing with market research in general and results and evaluations in particular.

Evaluations especially are often interpreted at will. Test results are taken as the final decision about communication, no second thought; individual results are ripped out of context or are overinterpreted on a whim. They simply lack a measure by which strengths and weaknesses can be defined. And this is a basic flaw in evaluating communication. Even the popular SWOT analysis (Strengths, Weaknesses, Opportunities, Threats) does not differentiate between marginal and essential.

Methodical traps — even the most basic ones — are glossed over. Are the test subjects really those post-modern trendsetters defined in the briefing, or are they the same university students from the institute's file catalog? And in the end it is simply accepted that the market research institute offers unsolicited solutions during the presentations of their results.

WHY NOT?
NOTHING WRONG WITH HAIRDRESSERS RECOMMENDING VACATION SPOTS EITHER.

Research is conducted to gain more security, but it is conducted under such ridiculous time pressure that the supposed advantages get lost. For example, right before Christmas, a time when any institute would struggle to find test subjects. Let alone a specific target group.

The best results come from market research using very recent "real-time" polls, like the famous "exit poll" right after an election. These results are usually within half a percentage point, at least for the large political parties. But when the question is asked, the decision has already been made.

Polls about new product launches, however, are all about declarations concerning intended behavior. The difference between the "Marry me!" and the "I would probably marry you" is obvious. This is where polls become questionable. But it doesn't stop here.

Originally, von Matt wanted to become a market researcher instead of a copywriter. Despite an early snag in his market research experience, from which he is still recovering. In 1970, Switzerland conducted a national caucus and all high school seniors were recruited as pollsters. Von Matt was assigned a stretch of Langstrasse in Zurich's 4th district. Many of the people living there fear nothing more than being asked about their personal affairs.

At almost every door there was so much obvious trickery, deceit, and lying that the truth was irreparably skewed. A boy who was at most 14 claimed to be an adult. A Kosovo-Albanian's name was Zuberbühler. A young lady in silk work attire was a marine biologist. He had to report countless implausible facts. To this day, von Matt is plagued with a bad conscience, but also with a healthy mistrust of polls of any kind.

WHY IS McDONALD'S SO CROWDED, EVEN THOUGH NOBODY EATS AT McDONALD'S?

Why is prostitution a thriving economic sector, even though almost no men take advantage of this service?

Because polls inevitably lead to slanted results. Few people like to expose themselves. Most want to seem, when asked, like thoughtful, intelligent, likeable people. They achieve this feat by orienting themselves with the majority. People want to belong, not stand apart, no matter what part of town they live in.

When asked which party he will vote for, the Schill voter doesn't respond "Schill." Only the anonymity of the voting booth allows him to say so. The consumer who gets polled about packaging suggestions acts exactly the same way. He chooses the product he believes the majority will choose, the most traditional one. Only the anonymity of the supermarket allows him to follow his own taste. And he picks whatever his heart desires most.

Of course, we don't intend to vilify market research. We've been able to profit from those informative results for too long. You can never know enough about your target group, its lifestyle, its buying and media behavior, or its fields of interest. And it certainly is immensely helpful to know whether certain conceptual approaches, brands, products, or services can be dramatized to fall on fertile ground within the defined target group. But:

YOU MUST KNOW WHAT YOU WANT TO KNOW AND WHAT YOU WANT TO DO WITH THAT KNOWLEDGE.

Tests can certainly help advertisers. They can provide leads about whether a campaign is really understood as intended. They can show whether a certain target group is addressed in a way that piques its interest. They can show if the general direction is right. But tests are of no use at all if advertisers blindly take results as recommendations.

No decision maker in the car industry would base design decisions merely on a so-called "Car Clinic." But that is exactly what happens in most cases when campaigns are tested.

Everyone knows that really outstanding designs—those that proved to have high momentum and became classics—usually met with initial rejection. Because they were different, because

WIRTSCHAFTSWOCHE "HONECKER," PRINT 1999:
HEADLINE: "EVERY FUSION HAS ITS SHARE OF LOSERS." WHO'S TO SAY THAT YOU CAN ONLY USE LIKEABLE, SUCCESSFUL PEOPLE TO ADVERTISE AN ECONOMICS MAGAZINE! TO WIT, THE THEME "NOTHING IS MORE THRILLING THAN THE ECONOMY." WEEK AFTER WEEK WE DEVELOPED A LONG-STANDING CAMPAIGN WITH NEW, ALWAYS THRILLING TAGLINES.

STOCK AGENCY: ARCHIV FÜR KUNST UND GESCHICHTE

no one was prepared. And advertising has to be even more surprising than design, since the naked messages of advertising are rarely really innovative and fascinating.

When a surgeon prepares for an operation he knows exactly what to expect after the incision. A matter of life and death for the patient. He knows where to operate, which instruments to use, and has enough knowledge to recognize what is going on in the patient's body. The surgeon knows the operative field intimately before he wields a scalpel. Market research institutes must know their operative field equally well—a matter of life or death for their product.

MARKET RESEARCH,
DRUGS
AND
WEAPONS
HAVE ONE THING IN COMMON:

They are not intrinsically bad—it all depends how you use them. Freely quoted from controversial German filmmaker Rosa von Praunheim, one could say, "It is not the advertising test which is perverse, but the world in which it exists."

And misuse is practically a given. Sure, since market research doesn't deal with rational insights but with a purely emotional need: security. And too often security is not just about a particular decision, but, sadly, about one's own career in the company.

Hindsight is 20/20 when campaign decisions are questioned after the fact. Everybody always knew better and everybody could clearly see that the campaign would never work. This decision climate is basically crying out for a security policy, and that is why market research, particularly pre-testing, is such a delicate topic.

One flaw of the market research tools normally in use is rooted in the fact that spoken communication is more limited than non-spoken communication. There are things that simply don't fit into our template for grammatical expression, and that have to be grasped by something other than language. An image (especially a moving image) is a medium with its own power of expression that simply can't be replaced by mere words.

The essential problem of understanding images, the reception of TV commercials, print ads, etc., is the transfer of a non-linguistic into a linguistic medium. But that is just what interview subjects are asked to do. In a conceptual test, the visual emotional meaning of an image is often supposed to be transformed into language-based expression that then becomes the subject of the evaluation.

It is our opinion that the images cannot be adequately described with words. Language fails to convey what images can: the expression of the inexpressible. "The picture shows a chalkstone cliff—obviously on the coast of the island Rügen in the Baltic Sea" does not provide a reliable description of the total experience of looking at a painting by Caspar David Friedrich.

Because images also contain non-verbal elements, these elements must be polled with equally non-verbal expressive means.

It is the only way to address the emotional components of the recalled media experiences. Market research has yet to provide a set of tools for this purpose.

Of course, middle management is in a difficult position in those companies where it is authorized to say no in terms of communication, but is never allowed to utter a decisive yes. Particularly when gutsy sidesteps are concerned. If it works, everyone simply says you did a good job, and the entrepreneurial laurels are reaped by others. If it fails, everyone says you don't have a clue about your job. So why fool around with unnecessary risks?

This is where a fundamental question of advertising communications comes into play. Is communication always the boss's business? One thing is certain, communication is too expensive and delicate to hand it over to just anyone. It deserves the best minds (or guts) in the business. On the other hand, communication issues demand intensive work and feeling. They cannot simply get a nod of approval—like other investment decisions—after one minute of looking at the numbers. Our first Audi presentation was important enough for Mr. Piëch to voice his own opinion. And he took his time. He obviously knew advertisers' bad habit of presenting something in the raw and later interpreting it any way they please. He insisted on the campaign appearing exactly as presented.

Communication should only be the boss's concern if it is considered a serious mission. Otherwise it is better that a person with the appropriate time and talent takes control. Someone who is still authorized to make decisions. Even if it is not the entrepreneur who decides, communication is an entrepreneurial topic through and through.

And entrepreneurial decisions should not be built on sand. But how can the opportunities that market research provides be utilized to make communication more efficient? Or to make more efficient communication? Here are a few insights from our experience.

Let's start with pre-testing. Truly new and innovative brand launches are too much for pre-testing tools. This is probably due less to the tool's shortcomings and more to the people questioned. We only accept something new when it has a special meaning for us. This does not immediately become apparent in something really new, but only in the framework and environment of a concerted effort.

For Audi, we were supposed to pre-test TV spots with a markedly new orientation. In the spot "Perfume," for example, in which an elegant woman pours expensive perfume in the radiator. The interview subjects felt that the chasm between the new attitude of the Audi brand and the traditional image of the brand was too wide to bridge. The new launch was absolutely unbelievable. And due to the sway of this unbelievability, the TV concepts were all flatly rejected. If such test results were taken seriously, all brand re-launches would be doomed to fail.

What is scornfully known as "illustrative marketing"—advertising concepts that literally convert a marketing concept without any creative input—is easily understood and accepted in pre-tests, but doesn't create much momentum in the marketplace. If you want to demonstrate your likeability you are well advised not to telegraph it literally. But to demonstrate it surprisingly and convincingly.

Clichés are an easily understood way to tell your subjects where a company's brand is headed. And this ease of understanding is always rewarded with positive evaluations and likely acceptance of the presented concepts. Anything surprising that leads to a more intense confrontation is always irritating.

This is where the infamous Advertising Manager Syndrome sets in. On the way from the street corner to the test studio, the test subject mutates from a completely normal person to I-have-to-seem-clever-because-I-am-being-interviewed Man. He switches from emotional to rational and says things like "I get it, but no one out there will."

Let's not forget, anyone willing to be a subject in a test session wants to seem intellectually agile. And he will ask himself the meta-question, "What does the institute want to accomplish with this advertising and the consumer?" Instead of seeing himself as the targeted consumer. The solution is easy:

> WE SHOULD LISTEN TO WHAT PEOPLE SAY,
> **BUT NOT SAY WHAT THEY WANT TO HEAR.**

Emotions are often the central issue, particularly those specific emotions targeted to be attached to a brand. In pre-tests, which, as we know, are intended to avoid misguided production costs before a campaign is set in motion, the test subjects' imagination is tickled rather clumsily.

How is a normal person — one who is confronted daily with an all-round onslaught of perfectly staged emotional messages — supposed to have his emotions triggered by cheap cartoons (animatics), unfamiliar story book techniques (storyboards), more or less successful explanations by MR moderators, or newly edited layout films (steal-o-matics)? Is he supposed to be moved so deeply that he is willing to like, love, buy a brand?

In Hollywood, studios even test which story endings work better for the audience. But in a perfect mise-en-scène. The finished movie is simply edited and shown in different versions. And then the audience has to choose how they will be entertained. In marketing pre-tests, they have to choose how they will be seduced. And there's a big difference.

Gutsy ideas — especially when they are politically incorrect — are frequently rejected because of the pressure that goes along with making a quasi-public statement. In individual as well as group polls. The pressure to defend yourself when you go against the established point of view, even in the mundane terrain of advertising, is often just too strong. It is also difficult to estimate the power of humor in an improvised setting. It always amounts to a detailed explanation of a joke, and the subsequent question:

WOULD YOU HAVE
LAUGHED?

JUNG v.MATT

SPARKASSE "MY HOUSE, MY CAR, MY BOAT," TV SPOT 1995:
ONE OF THE COUNTLESS SCRIPTS LIFTED DIRECTLY FROM VON MATT'S LIFE. HE ATTENDED A HIGH SCHOOL REUNION AND GOT ANGRY ABOUT ALL THOSE PICTURES THE OTHERS SHOWED HIM. MOST OF ALL BECAUSE HE DIDN'T HAVE ANYTHING TO SHOW HIMSELF. BUT HIS ANGER INSPIRED HIM TO WRITE A SPOT THAT FAR SURPASSED ALL OF SPARKASSE'S RECALL QUOTAS.

Creative suggestions are unavoidable in any kind of test. Either because everybody likes to play the smart advertising man, like a smart soccer coach or politician. Or because, in light of the represented opinion, it is unavoidable to talk about alternatives, interpretations, or improvements on the test concepts. Sure, this can inspire some new ideas, but should not be taken too seriously.

Here is a common case. A campaign is tested and one of the images proves to be the clear winner. Now the agency analyzes this winner and tells the creative team to "Play it again, Sam!" And it will fail.

Every time an artist tries to repeat his biggest success, it fails. The true creative greats never repeated themselves. Bach could have said, "The Brandenburg Concertos were my biggest hit, I'll just write something along those lines." Advertisers get this demand all the time.

If pre-testing is so limited, what might be useful for finding truth ahead of the game? In our experience, concept tests have served us well. If we don't test the mise-en-scène, we can at least present the communicative gist in concept tests. The message in its purest form. This is not possible, however, if the mise-en-scène is inseparably intertwined with the message. In the Sixt campaign, for example, where simple price offers would seem hardly exciting in the context of a concept test. But would be winning and exciting in the Sixt tonality.

But it was helpful in other product fields. For a well-known household disinfectant, for example. The polled subjects chose the following variant from a wide variety of offers: "You don't have to be a hypochondriac, and our immune system needs a little dirt to stay fit anyway, but in certain situations this product is really useful."

After the test yielded more security for this basic message, it was simpler to come up with creative ideas for this offer. And the following decisions about the campaign were easier as well. The goal was clear, as was the consumer's attitude towards the product. It was possible to make objective decisions. You didn't mean to aim at the master but hit his dog instead. Which is often the case when message and mise-en-scène are discussed all at once.

The general rule is, the more distinctly individual elements of a communication effort are tested, the more transparent, unambiguous, and constructive is the insight. This holds especially true for the basic analysis and evaluation of communication.

The effect of campaign and brand image should be monitored constantly. If a set of tools is installed and maintained over many years, it is possible to gain valuable insights about how to treat a brand in terms of communication.

Efficiency can be gauged more easily if it is possible to see whether advertising was perceived and whether any changes to the brand image occurred in a given timeframe.

It also becomes easier to weight the influence of other marginal conditions such as the brand's media status, certain developments inside the company that might influence the brand, as well as social and political influences.

No single market research measure can come close to the depth of the insights culled from monitoring ads and tracking images. After a zero curve at the beginning, a constant test design, and at least four polling cycles with at least 200 subjects annually, all decision makers get a feel for the brand's status in consumers' consciousness. And most of all for how the brand develops over time.

By the way, whenever opportunities for profit sharing in an agency are discussed, opportunities for concrete profit and goal agreements arise. Ideally, both monitoring and tracking are established, which are independent of each other in polling mode. It is easier to interpret the results because test subjects are not prone to follow any direct interpretative conjunctions of advertising and brand image. It is possible to take a relaxed look at how advertising was perceived and what was happening with the brand.

This can lead to baffling results. Our TV spot "My house, my car, my boat" for the savings bank Sparkasse not only created a catchphrase but also led to excited discussions a few days after it was first broadcast. The spot was deemed politically incorrect. Not just because it glorified superficial consumerism, but because the phrase "my groom" was perceived as hostile towards women.

Luckily, image tracking could prove the spot's momentum. Confidence in Sparkasse's investment competence increased significantly. Particularly among women.

CHAPTER 11

PENETRATION AND PERSISTANCE: UNEQUAL BROTHERS
ABOUT SIZE IN COMMUNICATION

Alain Prost was a great racecar driver. He drove in big races and was celebrated big time afterwards. But he also made some big mistakes. Then, the 166 cm tall man was a giant loser in everyone's eyes. When Edith Piaf, the barely 155 cm tall singer, died, the newspapers wrote, "The great Piaf is dead."

So, why are we almost always disappointed when we meet someone famous in the flesh? Because we imagined him or her to be "larger than life." If you ever have the chance to be face to face with Madonna or Maradona, you will notice a surprising difference. It is not the difference between you and the star. But between your image of the star and reality.

When you describe a person, you usually mention height and what we call figure. Height is a factor in a career. Height inspires trust. Just like Little Red Riding Hood trusts the wolf in the fairytale, you trust tall people more than short ones.

Tall people bring out submissive, primeval instincts in the rest of us. And the tall person feels he is tall. He has the natural advantage of an elevated point of view. And in "Short People" and "Little Criminals" Randy Newman comments ironically on the shortcomings of others.

PENETRATION AND PERSISTANCE: UNEQUAL BROTHERS

Size undoubtedly has a content dimension too. Big news, big events, and big successes. What is meant is important news, important events, and important successes. More than anything, size equals importance.

Everyone knows that whatever is printed in big letters in the newspaper is important. Whatever appears in small print doesn't matter much. Everyone can see it every day. Whatever the evening news reports for several minutes is of worldwide importance. Whatever gets mentioned only briefly is comparatively unimportant.

If Bild-Zeitung has a huge headline on page one, "Schumi in Accident," right away you think something terrible happened. If the same text is in small print, you think perhaps Michael Schumacher bent his front spoiler during test runs.

SIZE CHANGES CONTENT,

no matter whether it is in Bild-Zeitung or F.A.Z. The physical law of communication says "The size is the message."

When the Chancellor's Office was dedicated in Berlin, the size of the building was criticized. The reunified Germany would represent itself with an administrative complex too big, too expensive—in short, too monumental. But size becomes the insignia for power. The meaning changes and the respect also grows.

Churches and Jil Sander stores are built with lofty ceilings to make people feel small. High ceilings suggest respect and—in the true sense of the phrase—the highest regard. And this high regard brings measurable success. There must be something profitable in building showrooms more than two stories high, which devours a lot of rent and energy.

Why is it so hard for advertisers to follow this law? Why don't they recognize that their product or brand message will seem more important in a large format? Why don't they jump at this simplest chance to generate higher momentum? Because most advertisers think in frequency. In mistrustful anticipation, they assume that their message is so uninteresting that is must be repeated as many times as possible.

Even if repetition is doomed from the beginning. Every morning, thousands of frequent flyers are subjected to explanations about how to fasten their seatbelts and where, in the unlikely event of cabin pressure loss, oxygen masks will drop from the ceiling. Air travel regulations require this announcement, but nobody listens.

Everyone is disappointed when a lecture turns out to be a repeat. No one likes to listen to worn-out theses. Jung pouts every time something is repeated two or three times in a meeting:

> WHAT DO YOU THINK I AM, SENILE?

Why should consumers react differently if they are told the same thing six times in one night of television?

No newspaper editor would demand that a fascinating article

be printed six times. No TV station can stand out by reruns alone. The ratings will drop with every broadcast. And the station's image will suffer. Still, most advertisers try to maximize the frequency of their ads.

There are only two kinds of advertising where this really makes sense. Advertising for a brand that needs a constant media presence. And advertising that is so boring that it can only be placed in the context of brainwashing. How desperate! Dark throbbing drumbeats until the consumer gives up his resistance. Right along the lines of what German soldiers said after the war: "The Russians were stupid but there were just too many of them."

We have a clear opinion about the old dilemma of format and frequency. We believe that advertising must be an experience that the consumer has with a brand. If this experience is strong, one is enough. If it is weak, even ten won't do.

THE CONSUMER FEELS,
BUT HE DOESN'T KEEP COUNT.

Our client Sixt had this insight early on. From their first ad, it was all about the brand's ambition to become a market leader. Small formats were never an option. From the beginning the brand was never meant to be perceived as a cautious explorer but as the alpha dog. To make this strategy work, all their efforts were directed at the target group, business travellers.

PENETRATION AND PERSISTANCE: UNEQUAL BROTHERS

The old demand for communicative ubiquity needs some rethinking. In our communication-driven society it has become quite difficult, even with impressive budgets, to be present everywhere at all times. The competition — especially with regard to the media — has become too fierce. Penetration by persis-tence must be replaced by momentum. And momentum is inextricably connected with thinking in highlights.

Von Matt learned at the tender age of nine that this way of thinking wasn't just about content but about form as well. Graziella was adored by all the boys in the class. Von Matt was smitten too and tried to communicate this to her in some way. So he took the usual slip of paper and wrote "I would like to go steady with you."

Graziella immediately tore the paper up right in front of him. Others might have come up with more imaginative text at this point. But von Matt decided to optimize the medium and wrote the same text on a piece of cardboard. But Graziella tore this message up too. The next morning, von Matt came to school — not depressed, but in a great mood. He opened his backpack and handed Graziella the familiar message, this time on a wooden board. She smiled. And von Matt was very satisfied with his communication coup.

Maybe that was his eye-opener in terms of creative mediality, but he had learned something for sure — that you can place a message more effectively if it comes as a surprise to the recipient. Surprising details have a special seductive power. And our business is seduction.

Hier eine Liste aller Einwohner, die ihre Fernsehgebühren nicht bezahlen:

DEUTSCHE STÄDTE-MEDIEN "TELEVISION FEES," BILLBOARD 1994:
HEADLINE: "HERE IS A LIST OF ALL VIEWERS WHO DON'T PAY THEIR TV FEES." INSTEAD OF NAMES THE POSTER FEATURED THE FOLLOWING MESSAGE MANY THOUSANDS OF TIMES: "POSTERS MAKE YOU CURIOUS." WE DIDN'T JUST WANT TO CLAIM THAT EXTERNAL ADVERTISING CAN BE EFFECTIVE. WE ALSO WANTED TO PROVE IT LITERALLY TO THE MEDIA DECISION-MAKERS. THE CAMPAIGN BECAME AN EVENT — MANY RADIO AND TV STATIONS REPORTED ON IT EXTENSIVELY.

PENETRATION AND PERSISTANCE: UNEQUAL BROTHERS

Many advertisers think that the meaning of an advertising message is contained within the products and services themselves. That's good and certainly shows self-confidence, but it is only partly true. Products and services or, more generally, things, do not contain meaning within themselves like one Russian matroshka doll contains another.

But does "meaning" mean anything, and where does it come from? Meaning is created only because people are capable of comparison. No driver would think of comparing the meaning of traffic signs based on size or weight. However, people always think of company executives as having large offices and riding in large limousines. At least the successful ones. The category for differentiation is the allotted space. If our expectations are not met, we are at the very least surprised.

The simplest way of differentiation in advertising is size. As soon as we can tell products apart from each other, we can attribute different meanings. A large format is helpful in a simple but quite effective way.

For advertising, this means that the full-page ad and the 20-second standard commercial spot only satisfy our typical expectations of advertising. But they don't contribute anything to making products or services distinguishable, let alone attributing any special meaning.

Perhaps that is also the reason why it seems so difficult to create or accept something really new. Anything that tears apart the unity of word and image, imagination and name, seems irritating. The earth is flat, a spot is 20 seconds long, and an ad is full page. But isn't the irritating, the unusual a prerequisite for differentiation? And isn't differentiation the prerequisite for a distinctive attribution of meaning?

High frequency cannot compensate for lack of meaning. Frequency triggers exactly the opposite of meaning. If you repeat something constantly, you actually weaken and show the irrelevance of the message every time it appears.

Every child learns quickly that things that are important to the listener (him) only have to be said once to be understood. "Tomorrow you don't have to go to school." Things that are unimportant have to be repeated constantly:

"ELBOWS OFF THE DINNER TABLE."

Ever since there have been ambitious advertisers, they have tried to convince their clients to go with large formats. But it is often a pointless fight. The problem is that the recall formula doesn't work. A double-page ad usually costs twice as much as a full-page ad. But it only generates 1.6 times the recall value. The connection between ad format and viewing time or mail-in response is not quite linear.

So, advertisers sought refuge in qualitative argumentation. They said: A generous format makes the brand look bigger. A generous format makes the brand appear superior. A generous format expresses self-confidence and decisiveness, which reflects positively on the image.

It was our ambition to add a quantifiable result to this discussion. And we commissioned a spectacular test for that purpose. The thesis was that recipients of an advertising message attribute more meaning to that message if it is communicated in a larger ad or a longer TV spot. We wanted to capture this qualitative trend quantitatively.

It is easy to see a positive connection between format and attribution of meaning. But that wasn't enough. We wanted to prove with numbers:

HOW MUCH SIZE
YIELDS HOW MUCH INCREASE IN MEANING?

Our first attempt focused on editorial content. We showed our test subjects a fictitious news program without sound. One of the news items was a plane crash, documented with one of those typical pictures of wreckage. The important thing was that the picture didn't allow any deduction about the size of the plane. The image simply had the caption "plane crash." The first version showed this image for only 5 seconds. The second showed it for 30 seconds.

Then we polled our subjects. All 60 of them could recall the news about the plane crash. Then came the important question, "How many victims were there?" The 5-second group came up with an average of 28. They must have assumed a smaller plane or a private jet.

The 30-second group came up with an average of 110. They

instinctively assumed a large commercial plane. The test encouraged us to research further. In our second test we wanted to prove that the attribution of meaning also changes for an advertising message.

We created two ads each for four brands. One of them was a one-page, the other a double-page ad. Then the ads were incorporated into a popular magazine. The test subjects were asked to browse through the magazine and answer one question per pair of ads. For the first pair, the question was about the size of the company in terms of the number of employees; for the second, about the page number in a magazine; for the third, about the engine's horsepower; and for the fourth, about the amount of units in a distribution network.

And surprise! In every case, the larger ad actually yielded higher numbers. More momentum. On average, the test subjects' answers for the double-page ad were about 1.6 times higher than for the single-page ad. The figures prove for the first time that doubling the format size is more efficient. Not only does it yield 1.6 times the impact but also 1.6 times the attribution of meaning.

Suddenly a double-page ad is a good deal! If a double-page ad is associated with a substantially higher meaning, we are in a qualitatively different situation. Certainly there is room for improvement, additions to the polling population or in elements of the study design. But the result shows a tendency. And thus puts an end to the clueless blabber about greater superiority and stronger image impact.

PENETRATION AND PERSISTANCE: UNEQUAL BROTHERS

We are proud to have enriched the discussion of formats with a concrete figure. And we have less tolerance for small formats than ever before. If you want to belong to the club of the meaningful, you must afford a meaningful format. Communication is like an upscale cocktail bar:

THERE'S A TWO-DRINK MINIMUM.

Of course, this recommendation has a natural limit, the poverty limit. Not everyone can afford large formats. But even the advertiser with the famous "limited" budget has reasonable ways to make his ads seem larger.

Ironically, it is often easier to convince a small advertiser to go large than a Big Spender. People who command a 100 million euro budget generally think more quantitatively. They tend to be greater number crunchers than those who already have a tight budget and tend to say "If we do this, let's go all out!"

Unfortunately, advertisers with modest means are often influenced by the basic Big Spender rules and get scared off. We believe that all the basic rules concerning media planning are wrong. There is no minimum budget for TV advertising. There is no minimum frequency for print ads. There are only misleading averages from media researchers that don't help much in individual cases.

Is it wrong if a TV spot appears only once before a Formula One award ceremony and reaches 8 million car fanatics? Is it wrong if a TV budget is used to place trailers before every major league basketball game? Not at all. What is wrong is standard thinking in communication.

Besides frequency and format we keep wondering why clients invest a lot of money to find a creative angle for their ad concept but, at the same time, seem to be completely indifferent when it comes to creative angles in media planning.

Why do TV spots have to be 20 or 30 seconds long? Why does everyone demand and offer the "accepted" standards? 85% of all German TV spots conform to the German Industry Standard. Which results in the numbingly uniform rhythm in commercial blocks.

If the length of a TV spot is prescribed at 30 seconds — as happens so frequently in briefings — our creative teams get rebellious, and rightfully so. Let's think about a 60-second spot! Or a 5-second spot! Or how about 32 seconds? Or ten times 3 seconds?

The "standard" length of spots was not born out of random avarice. It has historical roots. It is a relic from an era when media use and media variety were completely different.

Let's walk down memory lane. Until the second half of the 1980s, advertising time was restricted to the public, state-owned TV channels. During that time broadcasters in the budding private sector were busy creating favorable conditions for federal programming regulations in order to receive broadcasting licenses.

DEA "SUPERINGO," TV SPOT 1998:
 NONE OF OUR TV CAMPAIGNS RECEIVED HIGHER RECALL VALUES
 THAN THOSE FOR DEA. BUT THE "SUPERINGO" SPOT BEAT THEM ALL.
 EACH SERIES HAS A HIGHLIGHT THAT MUST BE FEATURED
 EXTENSIVELY. OUR CLIENT INTERRUPTED THE RHYTHM OF THE
 DEA SITCOMS TO ACHIEVE THE MAXIMAL EFFECT FROM THIS SPOT.

DIRECTOR: OTTO ALEXANDER JAHRREISS
PRODUCTION: COBBLESTONE

PENETRATION AND PERSISTANCE: UNEQUAL BROTHERS

By 1987, the German Interstate Treaty on Broadcasting provided a framework for state media laws. TV commercials could now be placed with private TV channels. These providers became attractive because they suddenly increased area coverage and broke up the broadcasting monopoly. A media revolution began.

The station RTL plus—as it was then called—acquired the rights for major league soccer and Wimbledon. Until then, TV ads placed with the two big state-subsidized channels, ARD and ZDF, were restricted to the window between 6 p.m. and 8 p.m. Both channels got their revenue mainly from viewers' mandatory monthly fees. The basic TV programming mission entrusted to them didn't allow for greater commercialization.

Any ad placement request had to be submitted by September of the previous year. Then the available ad space was distributed. Newcomers were allotted 90 seconds per month. Large, continuously contributing advertisers were given preferential treatment.

It was like a promising Initial Public Offering. Every advertiser signed up—come what may—to get the highest possible ad allotment. And you had to run a tight ship with whatever ad space was handed out.

Fortunately, ad time is no longer this rare. Today, you can get everything, or nearly everything. Of course, there are still certain broadcast time slots and locations that are in high demand and get booked very quickly. But other than that, the medium of television can and must be treated the way the illustrated press once was. Ads must be planned and booked according to the environment they appear in. In other words, it is finally possible to book according to target groups and interests! Which means that, finally, specific segments can be addressed — even in this most emotional of all media — that would have been lost to dispersion in the early years of TV.

It is no longer important to be stingy with your TV budget; it is important to make a quality showing. Momentum doesn't go well with advertising's buckshot approach. It requires sharpshooters.

MANY CAMPAIGNS
WITH EXTRAORDINARY
MOMENTUM
ARE BASED ON UNUSUAL
FORMAT IDEAS.

Von Matt had one of his first unusual format ideas at the beginning of the 1980s. A shoe chain had split up its advertising budget into the usual mix: some daily papers, some cinema, some bus ads, some posters, etc. Von Matt recommended to the decision-makers that they concentrate their entire budget on a single medium. Bus ads, to be precise. This created the most spectacular bus advertising Germany had ever seen. Every bus had its own text. And every third bus in the city was advertising shoe stores.

When we had the opportunity to represent DEA, we were looking for a format that focused on the brand's first-class customer orientation and service.

We borrowed the format of TV sitcoms—small anecdotes at a gas station with a set cast of characters: Mr. Ahrens and his daughter, Ingo, Mrs. Tschernoster, Granny Buhl, and Dr. Eisendraht. This motley cast won over the hearts of the target group, which could be gleaned from the campaign's huge effectiveness ratings.

It was a lot like a real sitcom. We filmed the spots in seasons. And when the actor who played the gas station owner suddenly ambushed us with demands for a higher salary, we wrote him out of the series and replaced him:

MR. AHRENS BECAME MR. BEHRENS.

The sitcom idea didn't just require the DEA advertising team to leave the familiar 30-second format. We couldn't even tell them exactly how long each TV spot would last. But both the client and their surprisingly cooperative media agency agreed to an average length of 40 seconds.

In the eyes of the experts, it was sacrilegious when we presented, in all seriousness, a 60-second spot for our client Audi. But when the spot "Maharadja" ran and everyone felt the excitement this micro-movie created in the commercial blocks, they were quickly willing to raise the budget in order to give the spot even more visibility. It was one of the first spots on German television that looked like an opulent movie.

Our BMW campaign also began with an unusual format. We convinced BMW to make each ad a several-page event. The ad sequence seemed like an editorial sequence. When the campaign began, von Matt asked his father whether he had seen our BMW ad in Spiegel magazine. His answer was "No, I read something interesting about BMW but I didn't see your ad."

The desire to impress isn't always about large formats. Location can also surprise the consumer. And the way in which it is done. At the end of the 1970s the Kuschelweich brand produced a teddy bear as a self-liquidating offer that looked exactly like the one on the Kuschelweich package.

Jung was a young media planner at the time and needed to come up with a campaign to market this teddy bear as well as possible. Disregarding the traditional target group of housewives, he planned ads for the kid's magazine Bussi-Bär, in which the Kuschelweich bear was offered for sale. It was very successful.

Jung's first gutsy act of communication. It amounted to a revolution. Because the magazine wasn't even IVW-approved and so was completely outside of the usual media planning grid.

CHAPTER 12

A FIST IS STRONGER THAN FIVE FINGERS
ABOUT THE ADDED VALUE OF INTEGRATED CONCEPTS

In the late 1970s, an experimental post-punk band called The Plasmatics was tearing up the American music scene. One of their songs stuck with Jung. Not because it was a hit. It was an awful piece but it was based on an unusual idea. The five members of the band recorded the song in separate rooms. Without eye contact, and without being able to hear each other.

Many large brands unintentionally follow this example in their approach. Each of the many communication services instruments plays its own song and in the end there is chaos. Why does this happen? Everybody acknowledges the synergy of integrated communication.

> WHY IS SOMETHING
> THAT EVERYONE WANTS
> SO HARD TO ACHIEVE?

The first problem is a lack of awareness of the other channels. Very few communication services people think in network terms. Most of them concentrate on their special area and close their eyes when it comes to their neighboring disciplines. Of course there are also economic interests at play. Like a child making sure that his siblings don't get a bigger piece of the pie.

Then there is the problem of differentiation. Different agencies offer different communication services in different combinations. The advertising agency wants to create advertising but is happy to provide other services as well. It gets into fights with the PR agency over below-the-line job responsibilities. And lately there have been the new media agencies, claiming brand leadership for themselves and thus antagonizing all existing communication services providers.

Finally, there is leadership—the main problem facing integrated communication. Who takes the ideological lead of the brand?

The reason why integrated communication is less likely in large companies than in smaller ones is divided responsibility. The head of marketing is responsible for marketing. The head of communication services for PR. Both are competing with each other to some degree. Here is where the

FUNDAMENTAL SPLIT OF COMMUNICATION

originates, and it continues all the way to the bottom. The head of promotion will not take orders from the head of advertising. The Web master wants to push for his own agency preference.

Only one thing can help. Responsibility for communication must be pushed higher and higher until there is only one person left. The chairman of the board if necessary. Otherwise, there will never be integrated communication but only the opposite—concerted destruction of money.

Ironically, the one piece of communication usually handled by the chairman of the board, the one item for which he makes time and contributes his own ideas, is the company Christmas card. It appears to be especially important because he puts his own signature on it. Meanwhile, he forgets that exceedingly important pieces of communication, which don't just end up in the mailboxes of 100 business friends but reach millions of customers, are sent with a much more precious signature: his brand's.

Speaking of mailboxes. A few weeks after we won the account for Deutsche Post, the German postal service, Jung and von Matt each received a remarkable letter in the mail—from the Deutsche Post.

What was remarkable was not the content—it was a run-of-the-mill mass mailing for advertising purposes—but the form, language, and style. The entire mailing corresponded exactly to the layout and tonality of the campaign we had presented to the Deutsche Post people. Before our first piece of advertising was even published.

Obviously, there was someone in this company with the talent to orchestrate communication services measures so that everyone was playing the same piece. Within a very short amount of time. When we got to know Professor Gert Schuckies, former communication manager at Deutsche Post, we realized what this talent entailed. Consideration while evaluating communication. Determination while seeing it through. An exotic and rare combination.

BMW "HORSES," PRINT 2003:
THIS MOTIVE IS A GOOD EXAMPLE FOR BOTTOM-UP MARKETING. EVERYTHING STARTED WITH AN ADVERTISING IDEA: THE ENGINE POWER OF A BMW COULD BE REPRESENTED BY A HERD OF HORSES. THE IDEA HIT THE SPOT AND WE WERE ABLE TO CREATE A LOGICAL STRATEGY AROUND IT. EVENTUALLY, THE AD WAS USED INTERNATIONALLY.

PHOTOGRAPHER: MATS CORDT

A FIST IS STRONGER THAN FIVE FINGERS

A few decades ago, integrated communication was handled quite simply. Take a key visual, preferably an ad. With a headline shortened to a maximum of seven words it becomes a poster. With a modified headline and different text plus an excerpt from the media plan it becomes a trade magazine ad. The TV commercial also gets its key image from the original ad. Before we see the key image, the product is already being used or enjoyed in the commercial. If possible, with catchy music or a strong voiceover to create synergy with radio spots. Not bad.

With today's integrated communication, it is hard to shake the suspicion that the agencies are primarily concerned about the added value of each account. And not about powerful synergistic approaches.

Changing the center of gravity within the media certainly had an effect on integration behavior. The TV spot became the focus, with the print ad becoming the concentrated key scene.

No matter which medium you start with, the creative quality will suffer at some point.

THE ETERNAL
DILEMMA
OF MARKETING COMMUNICATION REMAINS:

A FIST IS STRONGER THAN FIVE FINGERS

SUBOPTIMAL INTEGRATION
OR
SUBOPTIMAL FASCINATION?

A fact that is actually not that surprising since every medium comes with its own specific requirements. Neglecting them means wasting the creative possibilities of using the medium according to its strengths. Integrated communication simply can't be seen in such a simplistic or, more importantly, such a formalistic way.

Anyone who doubts the value of integrated communications starts down a slippery slope. It is too obvious that everyone involved in the look of a brand—from the package designer to the media agency—must be absolutely in step with the others. It is all too obvious that a brand with a consistent look and spirit from Web site to shelf wobbler has a higher momentum than a brand with a hodgepodge of styles.

We have always followed the rules of our original discipline—classic advertising—with great passion and perfectionism. Sure, it kept bugging us when neighboring disciplines didn't pursue this "search for excellence." For example, when a beer brand—entrusted to us for classic advertising—started a direct marketing concept that was far below the creative level of our campaign. Or when an automobile brand's trade fair booth basically undermined our advertising appearance.

YOU KNOW WHAT HAPPENS IF YOU DON'T DO EVERYTHING YOURSELF.

NUR DIE "BUS," TV SPOT 2000:
ONE OF THE FAVORITE SPOTS ON OUR SHOW REEL. THIS SUCCESS WAS ONLY POSSIBLE BECAUSE THE CLIENT HAD THE COURAGE TO DEPART FROM THE USUAL STANDARDS, ADVERTISING A FASHIONABLE PRODUCT WITH A WOMAN WHO WAS NOT PARTICULARLY GOOD-LOOKING. UNFORTUNATELY WE HAD TO RETRACT THIS SPOT DUE TO A COMPETITIVE CONFLICT.

DIRECTOR: OLIVIER VENTURINI
PRODUCTION: TEMPOMEDIA

A FIST IS STRONGER THAN FIVE FINGERS

We started thinking about other communications disciplines. About a new media agency that doesn't just think about lucrative distribution systems but tackles creative tasks with enthusiasm. About a direct marketing agency that wants more from its addressees than maximum mail-in responses.

And also about a media agency that doesn't just crunch numbers but feels and fights for its principles. That doesn't just trudge along the comfortable standard paths but wants to break with the German Industry Standard of advertising.

It wasn't difficult to find people who supported this spirit. It wasn't easy, however, to find a system that could put the talent and ambition of those people on the same track. And make truly integrated communications possible. Following our tendency to name things according to their effect rather than their cause, we call this Cumulative Communication.

We knew that we could only move forward with an innovative process. New media came to our aid. At the core of our process was the "glass incubator," a separate area within our intranet where all participating disciplines could display their creative work. But transparency alone didn't help.

It was essential to find a way to manage timelines and leadership demands efficiently. Since such a process was inevitably charged with strong emotions, we aligned the phases to approximate the human search for a mate.

After the client briefing comes the "wooing phase" in which all communications disciplines, independent of each other, search for possible concepts. Simultaneously, the efficiency planners work on the strategy. During the "rendezvous" all the disciplines sit around a table and agree on the strategy and the main theme of the campaign.

As in real life, it sometimes takes a second rendezvous to get to the point.

Then comes the "going-at-it-like-rabbits phase" where all the disciplines search for concrete ideas based on the agreed concept. Here, the previously mentioned "glass incubator" provides the necessary transparency. Finally, at the "wedding," all the modules are combined into a consistent presentation.

If you enter the words "integrated communication" in a search engine, the German-speaking countries alone yield more than 10,000 service providers. These often reduce their creativity to inventing new synonyms that are sold to the client as a solution for a previously unknown challenge. "Networked communication," "360-degree communication," "complete solutions" are the magic words for improving efficiency.

There are, however, heated debates among experts about what actually distinguishes integrated communication, and the experts are hard pressed to reward it with actual awards.

A brand is a product that can be standardized to ensure

consistent quality. And it demands consistent quality in communication. The consumer is confronted with the brand in a large variety of situations. And he is supposed to experience the same effect, the same emotional values at each encounter. And always extend the same feelings towards the brand.

This began in the earliest days of marketing with product quality and consistency, brand equipment, price, and retail placement. And automatically applied to communications too. It was certainly easier at that time, since there was a clear overview of the media available.

The integration idea was directed towards the brand itself rather than being a specific challenge for communication.

Today, we are looking at a completely different situation. The media explosion, the entrance into the age of communication, exposes brands to the great danger of losing their orientation. Losing orientation does not mean simply committing formal mistakes and wasting the chance to make a brand instantly and unambiguously identifiable.

Losing orientation means diluting the brand's message. Integrated communication means two things for all channels: transmitting the content convincingly, and anchoring the sender effectively.

But the main challenge is not just bringing together the different communications disciplines. It starts within classic advertising.

A FIST IS STRONGER THAN FIVE FINGERS

ONE OF THE
BIGGEST PROBLEMS IN
CREATING ADVERTISING
IS THAT WE ARE ALL BASICALLY
CHILDREN OF THE PRINTED WORD.

We categorically think in print. It starts right at birth, which is announced in print. Our first drawing is print. Our first school notebook is print. Our first love letter is print. Even the money we earn is print. As are walking papers. And shortly after our death, another printed announcement.

Our entire life is accompanied and determined by print. Of course, it is in the theater that we watch the first movie that moves us to tears. And on TV that we cheer the first World Cup goal. But the serious side of life is in print.

Apparently, we don't lose this orientation if we happen to join a creative team in an ad agency. There is just no other way to explain why so many TV commercials look like filmed print ads. And so many radio spots sound like print ads read out loud. And most posters like enlarged print ads. And shelf wobblers like miniature print ads.

Once when von Matt stepped off a plane in Stuttgart he saw a huge billboard on the roof of the parking garage. Thanks to the main image he could guess that what was being sold was music systems for cars. But who was courting him? Blaupunkt? Sony? Alpine? Since he couldn't recognize the sender, he wasn't able to call the head of marketing to let him know that he needed a new agency. One who understood the essence of a billboard: bold, broad strokes.

No medium is designed badly as often as this simplest and oldest medium in the world. Just take a conscious look at billboards on your ride to the office. In our opinion, every other poster does not deliver its message. Many of them are plainly cheating the client because they have not been designed appropriately for the medium. The logo is too small, there is too much text, no clear image, it's all too complicated, etc.

Occasionally we get it wrong too, and you need a ladder and magnifying glass to decipher one of our billboards. And even though our creative director Deneke von Weltzien never tires of repeating his credo:

"ENLARGE THE LOGO UNTIL IT HURTS AND THEN
DOUBLE ITS SIZE!"

Good campaigns juggle the specific medium's possibilities perfectly. They make use of what that medium can do best. When von Matt is asked to be a panel judge in a billboard competition, he never fails to point out that "bold and broad" should be the main criteria for an award.

His vision is a competition where only these count. It takes place at a defunct airport. The competing billboards are placed at the end of the runway. The judges then walk slowly towards them. The first one that gets recognized wins.

A FIST IS STRONGER THAN FIVE FINGERS

On the other hand, unity is an expression of strength, security, dependability. It suggests that the stronger the bond between mother and father, the more respect is due to the child. Unity gives strength. In appearance as well. Soccer teams, armies, street gangs don't wear matching outfits for nothing.

British Airways once had a wonderful idea. They said, "Why don't we use our fleet to transport likeability?" They had different artists paint the exterior of their planes. But the effect was catastrophic—in polls the airline was judged to be cheaper, less safe, and more provincial. And the market share sank considerably until the mistake was corrected and the entire fleet was back in uniform.

Everyone can visualize these effects. A fist is simply stronger than five fingers. Why then is there so little willingness to work towards a uniform appearance?

The main problem of integrated communication is leadership. Who takes the lead? Who takes the first step?

The ad agency claims leadership. It says, "We have the most experience in brand leadership." The media agency demands leadership. It says, "We plan the media deployment for an ad campaign, and so we're right at the source of return on capital."

The new media agency wants leadership. It says, "The business of the future takes off from where we come into play." The company consultant claims leadership. He says, "Only I know exactly where this company's potential lies." And there are the

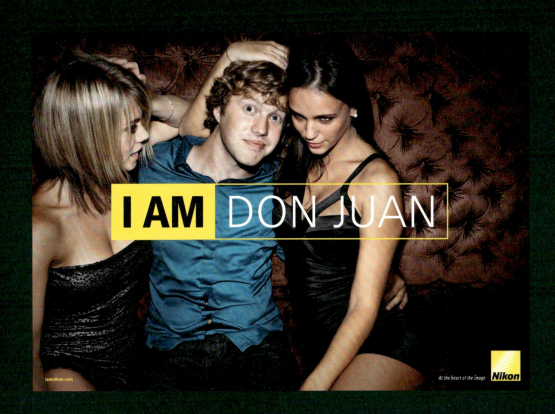

NIKON "COOLPIX," INTEGRATED CAMPAIGN 2010:
OUR TASK WAS TO OPEN UP THIS PROFESSIONAL PHOTOGRAPHY BRAND TO THE VAST TARGET AUDIENCE OF COMPACT CAMERA USERS. "I AM NIKON" WAS THE BASIS OF THE NIKON PRESENTATION IN TV AND PRINT, IN THE SOCIAL WEB MEDIA, AT THE POS AND AT PHOTO-KINA, THE WORLD'S LARGEST PROFESSIONAL PHOTOGRAPHY TRADE FAIR. AND IT WAS ADAPTED BY ALMOST ALL MARKETS WORLDWIDE.

PHOTOGRAPHER: SVEN JACOBSEN

package designer, the PR agency, and every other department who wants everything except to be led.

However, the creative people are also in a jam when faced with the demand for integrated communication. The chicken-or-egg question of creative teams is "Which medium takes the lead? Print or TV? Online or offline?"

During the boom of the New Economy there were frequent demands for the new media to take over brand leadership. Luckily, this spooky phase passed quickly, which prevented many big, beautiful brands from falling into the hands of digital technicians.

When we took over the account of the private TV station SAT.1, there was a meeting for everyone involved in the station's communications. For us, it ended with a shock. Fred Kogel, the station manager at the time, explained his wish for integration. In particular, the on-air communication that advertised the station itself during programs was supposed to collaborate with the off-air communication that was our responsibility.

We nodded gamely since we naturally assumed we could take over the leadership. But then we learned how our rather considerable 30 million euro budget fit into the big picture: it was less than 5% of the total SAT.1 advertising budget. The rest consisted of trailers, cross promotion, onscreen design, etc. We wanted to take the station's communication lead, but we were a nothing of barely 5%. The star was the 95% guy who designed the program trailers. We were extras.

There are few advertisers who force all disciplines to sit around the same table. And calibrate all communication channels regularly. One of our clients, DEA, had a jour fixe every month that includes at least the creative and media agencies. The Diebels brewery regularly brings PR and advertising agencies together. But in many large enterprises the different communication disciplines are so distinctly separate that they act almost like competitors.

It is frightening how little the specialists involved in creating the overall look of a brand communicate with each other. How frequently they work against each other because of colliding interests.

When von Matt met his wife ♥ who worked in the media business, he noticed that creative agencies and media agencies rarely communicated with each other. He accompanied his wife to media events and felt like a flower seller who had stepped up to a table full of blind people.

In all fairness, we must admit that media planners are not necessarily celebrated when they show up at creative festivals. Up to now, von Matt was sure of one thing: "We are the ones who do the advertising."

Suddenly he met people who were sure of this: "We are the ones who do the advertising." With the same condescending attitude. The creative people think of the media people as little bean counters, while they think of us as little image painters.

A FIST IS STRONGER THAN FIVE FINGERS

THERE IS TOO MUCH TALK AND TOO LITTLE DIALOG.

That is the reason why integrated creative media ideas are so rare. Whenever one materializes, it is immediately celebrated as a miracle.

When we were bored with the inevitable 30-second TV commercials and were looking, once again, for unusual ways to advertise for BMW, we hit upon the following idea. We wanted a car to drive through all the spots in an entire commercial block. At the edge of the screen, right through all the other commercials. Ads in the press were supposed to create attention for this advertising premiere.

It was not hard to win over the BMW people. Those clients who think in innovative ways are tired of the same old stanv dard formats too. And SAT.1 showed interest right away. They were also eager to participate in a new and spectacular idea to market ad space.

It was much tougher, of course, to negotiate this split screen with the station's other advertising clients. They had to accept that a car was driving underneath their commercials, which was eased by a 20% rebate towards the cost. And it certainly helped that the car was nothing less than a BMW.

In the end, we created a piece of advertising that received positive press and also showed a clearly higher attention level than conventional spots. And finally, it won the prestigious German Media Award.

The BMW block was a unique communication coup. But the fact that it was realized at all is due to pure coincidence. The coincidence that the creative guy who had the idea and the media girl who pushed the idea through in 14 companies were sharing a house and a bed: von Matt and von Matt.

The fault is in the system. As the media business keeps degenerating into pure mass business, it separates itself more and more from the creative business, which can only continue to make an impact through the quality of its creative and consulting services.

Both parties are equal players in the advertising industry and are not in any direct relationship or dependency. Since nothing is harder to find than a unique advertising idea, creation must take the lead in the content arena.

Whenever Jung comes to a place that is very, very expensive, he notices the high number of cash-paying Russians. Whether in a posh boutique in St. Moritz or in a top restaurant in Miami — there are always these funny-talking men with their fat wads of cash. Whenever he gets to a place that is very, very beautiful, he notices the high number of homosexuals. At the world's most exclusive beaches as well as in the most picturesque coffee houses. A special sense seems to lead these boys to places that the Average Joe wouldn't find right away.

But whenever he visits a place that is both very expensive and very beautiful, he is not likely to meet gay Russians but plain old media planners. Lots of them.

The explanation is banal. Publishing houses and TV stations pull out all the stops to keep their most important clients amused. And since the media competition has become tougher and tougher, they do even more. While we in our creative agencies are struggling late into the night to find better solutions, our partners on the media side are exquisitely wined and dined. And the next morning those people are supposed to dictate where our ideas generate the highest momentum?

CHAPTER 13

THE PEOPLE DETERMINE WHAT BECOMES A SLOGAN
ABOUT GOOD, BAD, AND NO SLOGANS

Even the Ancient Romans had the urge to publicize things, but there was no suitable media available. That's why the emperors issued coins that proclaimed great military victories or new concessions for the people. A symbol on the coin showed the event with a slogan such as "Freedom, equality, and justice."

Space was limited. The other side showed a picture of the emperor who had done the glorious deed. The goal was to improve his personal image, which explains why even a nobody among emperors, such as Antonius Pius, had more than 150 coins made per year.

Slogans originated due to lack of physical space. Today, they are used due to lack of space in the consumer's brain.

Almost every ad campaign running today contains a slogan or a claim. And at most, one out of a hundred achieve decent popularity. Most slogans are not worth their ink. They serve as an alibi to integrate disparate communication pieces, but serve no other function beyond that. They often are created out of pure routine, like the dutiful vicar who ends his sermon with "Amen." The dutiful advertiser ends his campaign with a slogan.

THE PEOPLE DETERMINE WHAT BECOMES A SLOGAN

That's why one should ask whether it makes sense to have a slogan at all. Can it contribute to a higher momentum? If not, the slogan can be cut altogether. Many big campaigns never needed a slogan to unleash this cumulative force. Others owed a large part of their effectiveness to a slogan.

The art of marketing communication is to use a message to transform external control over the consumer into internal self-control. If advertising only appealed directly to values and desires, it would not take long to recognize the attempt at manipulation. People want to feel that they can make their own decisions when they are addressed by advertising.

To achieve this, signs, language, and images must be used in such a way that they activate the consumer's own, very personal experiences. And also increase the recipient's willingness to form associations to the detriment of sound judgment.

Semiotics has proven that such demands are more easily fulfilled by images than by language, particularly if they appeal to the irrational. In other words, slogans are the intersection of language's ability to convey abstracts and an image's power to trigger associations. Slogans function as a relay station, as crankshaft and transmission.

Great slogans are advertising statements that become idioms. Or even simpler, great slogans are idioms. Just as popular and indestructible as: Hi y'all! The early bird gets the worm. A stitch in time saves nine. What's up? How's it hangin'? Holy crap!

Slogans also follow the laws of idioms, as simple thoughts that gain general acceptance in a surprising and attention-getting form. Plausibility on the one hand, remarkability on the other. In this case, remarkability is a prerequisite for retainability. In other words, a slogan is an "Oh, I see" event with a "Huh?!" effect. To put it as a slogan, "Huh?!-Oh-I-see!"

Just try to check the

HUH?!-OH-I-SEE! FORMULA

in familiar slogans. You will notice that you come up with many examples that are no longer current or actively used but are still effective. This too shows that nothing makes an advertising message last longer than a strong slogan.

Another reason why slogans have gained importance is that written culture has decreased. The global advertising world is in the middle of a manic trend towards the visual. Fun with language has become rare in advertising. We noticed, for instance, that automobile ads have basically lost their language. In 1975, they averaged 210 words, in 1985 they were down to 120 words, and in 1995, only 55 words.

In this case, advertising prematurely over-interpreted a trend. While most newspapers and magazines blithely make their living by the written word, advertising simply decided, "We won't write anymore." Thus, the slogan acquires an additional function as "ad text for lazy readers."

THE PEOPLE DETERMINE WHAT BECOMES A SLOGAN

A good slogan becomes a brand's communicative property, something difficult to erase from the consumer's consciousness or to separate from the brand.

Classic slogans even outlast generations of consumers. They pop up in every market research analysis about the respective brand. Even if they have long since been abandoned by the media.

Our soft spot for slogans goes along with respect for slogans that have proven their s(t)aying power in everyday use. When we were asked to develop a new communication concept for Jever beer, we came upon an old slogan that Jever had not used in years: Wie das Land, so das Jever, roughly, "Like the countryside, so is Jever."

We went to interview consumers to find out what was special about this slogan. It actually turned out to have a high retention effect, triggering positive nostalgic feelings in tradition-conscious beer aficionados. We proposed a revival of this slogan, which was convincing and has accompanied the brand to this day.

One day, von Matt was contacted by the inventor of the slogan—Horst Thomé, von Matt's mentor from his years at Ogilvy. Thomé became quite sentimental when he recounted how he had come up with the slogan decades before. He had been able to prevail against all concerns of the Jever people, who simply couldn't imagine that the quaint Northern German region of Ostfriesland could be the Unique Selling Proposition for a national beer brand.

THE PEOPLE DETERMINE WHAT BECOMES A SLOGAN

When in 1994 we had the chance to present a new campaign concept to the folks at Mediamarkt, an appliance and electronics retailer, we knew that a strong slogan would be important not only as a battle cry in a very aggressive market but also as a connective element in a widely-varied campaign.

The best we could come up with was "Calculated madness." But then we heard that our competitor had presented a real catchphrase: "I'm not stupid, you know." A wonderful slogan with all the features of a long-running hit. We knew that we had lost. And rightfully so.

We also had presentations where our idea for a slogan was accepted but the rest of our recommendations weren't. There are three well-known slogans for which our agency was only the surrogate mother.

The difficulty has always been, what is a slogan like that worth? Till Wagner, formerly working for Jung von Matt am Main, once asked for advice in this matter. Jung wasn't able to help him. But during that same phone call Wagner also mentioned that he was planning to add a second floor to the agency building that was supposed to cost 165,000 euros. And that's how the slogan got its price.

It is not easy to convince a client to go with a slogan if he has not been dealing with communication issues on a regular basis. Because a strong slogan, like a trendsetting car design, needs some time to catch on. Rule of thumb: if you like it right away, it will quickly lose its flavor. If it puzzles you at first, the flavor will last longer.

THE PEOPLE DETERMINE WHAT BECOMES A SLOGAN

For a long time we thought that "Maximum Excitement" was a good slogan for the new Mini. It was to the point, content-wise, and was suitable for international audiences. After all, we were supposed to find a phrase that would work in as many markets as possible worldwide. And we certainly couldn't go wrong with "Maximum Excitement." A typical slogan of the kind Jung likes to call:

TOO RIGHT TO BE GOOD ADVERTISING.

Only when Oliver Voss thought of "Is it love?" did we find the spirit of the car and the nerve of the audience. We noticed, not without pride, that the slogan was also used in Japan, Australia, and Tahiti, and that the press constantly quoted it in their reports about the car.

Since great slogans are at the core of a long-term plan, they must remain top secret. There is always the danger of a competitor finding out about it and throwing a curve ball. When Honda Motorcycles was planning to introduce the slogan "Follow the leader. He's on a Honda." in America, Yamaha's agency got wind of it and recommended a national campaign to begin exactly one week before the launch of the new Honda campaign. The slogan: "Don't follow anyone." With this coup, Yamaha won over freedom-loving motorcycle fans.

By the way, there are many slogans that were never supposed to be slogans. There are often other bits of text, particularly snippets of dialog, that accidentally achieve slogan-like penetration. Simply because the people want it that way. For instance, AOL's

THE PEOPLE DETERMINE WHAT BECOMES A SLOGAN

"Ich bin drin" (I'm online). Or the slogan for Clausthaler non-alcoholic beer: "Not all the time, but time and time again."

"My house, my car, my boat" became an idiom for possession as well. One night, Jung watched an interview with racecar driver Michael Schumacher. He answered the question if wealth was important to him by saying, "No, I'm not all about 'My house, my car, my boat'."

No one understands what matters in a slogan more than barkers at a farmer's market. No one listens to the voice of the people better than they do, because these advertisers play a double role. They are the medium and the message at the same time, and can thus get continuous feedback about the quality of their slogans.

A barker usually has nothing more to offer than the competitor right next to him. His advertised goods are no better or worse than those of his neighbor and are therefore not of particularly greater interest for the market consumers. Price also has a bottom limit, so they have to think of something else. That's why barkers have always felt the same pressure to differentiate as advertisers have.

And that's why the good old barkers act just like we do. They package their goods in humorous and mischievous monologues so people will stop, get intrigued, and buy something. Their rhetorical skills are legendary and can be witnessed at Hamburg's fish market, if you happen to be there at 6 o'clock on a Sunday morning.

MINI "FLIGHT CHART," PRINT 2001:
   WHAT COULD BE NICER FOR AN AGENCY THAN TO ADVERTISE
   A PRODUCT THAT EVERYONE WILL LOVE RIGHT AWAY? THE JOUR-
   NALISTS WERE DELIGHTED. AND EVEN HARDENED CAR TESTERS
   SHOWED SOME FEELINGS. THUS OUR SLOGAN FOR THE WORLDWIDE
   LAUNCH CAMPAIGN WAS ONLY LOGICAL: "IS IT LOVE?"

   PHOTOGRAPHER: DANIEL M. HARTZ/OLIVER RHEINDORF

THE PEOPLE DETERMINE WHAT BECOMES A SLOGAN

It is not easy to come up with rules for slogans. Because it is often by breaking the rules that a good slogan comes into being. Which means that every traditional rule about slogans has wonderful exceptions. Even the rule that a slogan should be short and sweet, derived from the post-war rhyme about a round loaf of bread that seemed to the poor man to be a luscious cake,

"WAS BEDARF ES VIELER WORTE, RING-BROT IST DER ARMEN TORTE"

and the long-running standard "Kids and grown-ups love it so! The happy world of Haribo!" to England's best known beer slogan "Heineken refreshes the parts other beers cannot reach."

However, there are a few guidelines that might help in writing or evaluating slogans.

First, you have to be aware of the following hierarchy. The copywriter decides which slogan makes it into the manuscript. The client decides which slogan makes it into the campaign. And the people decide if it really becomes a slogan.

Ergo, either a slogan touches the hearts of the people or it goes up in smoke. That's why slogans directed at a broad audience have so much trouble with clever wordplay or ironic exaggeration. Ambiguous phrases, in particular, have to face the following problem: 50% recognize meaning number one, 30% recognize meaning number two, and only 20% recognize the double meaning.

The exceptions are slogans that address opinion makers exclusively, and thus have an audience that knows how to read irony. One of the finest slogans of this species is one Scholz & Friends created for Baden-Württemberg, a Southern German state with a distinct accent and dialect: "We know how to do everything. Except speak German."

As far as penetration and recognition are concerned, a spoken slogan has a distinct advantage over anything written down. For decades, Germany's TV audience heard a sonorous voice reminding them that they were, "with any luck, Allianz-insured." This little caption in Allianz's print ads would have never had the same impact.

It is even easier for a sung slogan. But the jingle has to overcome the fact that singing weakens the content. And also reduces the value of the offer. Imagine the slogan for F.A.Z., "There is always someone smart behind it," set to a perky little ditty. And if that image is not clear enough,

> IMAGINE IF JOHN F. KENNEDY HAD SUNG "ICH BIN EIN BERLINER."

One of the basic conditions for a slogan to be effective is, of course, correct attribution. And incorrect attribution can be fatal in the sense that it can unintentionally favor the competition. Of course it doesn't hurt if the slogan contains the brand name.

For the (not really short, by the way) classic Esso slogan: "We've got a lot to do. Let's tackle it." there was a 35% incorrect attribution. Every one out of three costumers thought the slogan came from Esso's competitors Aral or Shell. Not a good return for such a long-term investment. On the other hand, the slogan "Go Nogger yourself" for the ice-cream bar had no trouble at all. Attributing slogans correctly is a popular game in the USA that is even offered via a Web site. But don't play this jolly guessing game with your kids. You won't stand a chance!

A slogan like "Just do it!" will certainly not leave questions about the sender within its target group. "Nothing is impossible" has been on air for too long to be falsely attributed to anyone but Toyota. And "The impossible furniture store from Sweden" is a clear link to IKEA. Both uniqueness and the consistency of a brand's appearance help to make a slogan immediately recognizable.

You often get the impression that a slogan gets pulled right before it becomes a familiar idiom. Because the strategy changes or—even more banal—the agency gets dumped. That is as painful as if you're drilling for oil and give up right before it starts to gush to go drill somewhere else. The fate of many great slogans that were missing just one thing—a decision-maker with an open mind.

When you are looking for a slogan, you have to be aware that

THE ART OF ADVERTISING IS NOT ABOUT
DEVELOPING A SLOGAN,
IT'S ABOUT DISCOVERING A SLOGAN.

If you give a bunch of third graders the task to write something about the mail-order catalog Otto-Versand, you shouldn't

THE PEOPLE DETERMINE WHAT BECOMES A SLOGAN

be surprised if "Otto... I like it" is the result. Most of the great slogans could have been written by elementary school students. "It's a Sony!" "Got milk?" "Have you driven a Ford lately?" But picking "Otto... I like it" out of hundreds of slogan suggestions and recognizing the momentum of this phrase—that's what creative gut feeling is all about.

You don't have to be sober to come up with a slogan like Bitte ein Bit! (A Bit, please!) for the beer Bitburger Pils. But you have to be very alert to recognize the potential of this everyday phrase. This is where the genius of the slogan finder comes in. The talent for looking through long lists and stopping right at the one sentence that will go right to the consumer's gut.

We have not met many people who can spot great slogans easily. This talent is rare even in agencies. And frequently even a list with a thousand suggestions doesn't have a single one with that special something.

Phrases that sound colloquial have an especially hard time in the cool, intelligence-laden environment of a formal presentation. When we presented the slogan "Joy, joy, joy is a fresh Diebels!" to the Diebels brewery, our greatest concern was to get some chuckles, as intended. Three months later, the slogan was known all over Germany and was inseparably linked with the brand—a feat none of the previous slogans was able to pull off, even after years of exposure.

Strong slogans can provide a campaign with a genetic code. If the DNA is healthy, success will rock the cradle. And if there are communication experts on the client's side, we can assume the code will be understood.

During the unveiling of "Bild Dir Deine Meinung!" (Form your own opinion!), our logo-incorporating, play-on-words slogan for Bild-Zeitung, something happened that is quite rare in big presentations. Just as the slogan appeared on the screen, one of the former editors-in-chief, Norbert Körzdörfer, blurted out:

"COOL!"

An unforgettable moment for Jung. He knew we had a hit. Of course, we were also confronted with client concerns. Is it proper to address the reader so informally? And: Isn't it presumptuous that Bild-Zeitung is billed as an "opinion-maker," when it is really the least likely source of reliable information? A reliable opinion poll extinguished any remaining doubts that the new slogan's intentional cognitive dissonance might be too jarring. Since its launch, this has become one of the best-known slogans around.

SAT.1 was also receptive when they heard our proposed slogan SAT.1, ich drück Dich! — another play on words in German, meaning both "SAT.1, I'm pressing your button (on the remote)!" and "SAT.1, I'm hugging you!" The trend video we provide with every creative recommendation showed an already polarized audience for this one. There were a few who rejected the idea. But what we cared about was that it emotionalized viewers. You could feel the fun people had with "Ich drück Dich!"

THE PEOPLE DETERMINE WHAT BECOMES A SLOGAN

An elderly lady spontaneously gave the interviewer a hug and didn't let go of him. But the slogan did not become a success because we didn't manage to turn it into an exciting campaign. And, most of all, couldn't find a way to use the slogan within the station.

The English phrase "Powered by emotion." has taken its place instead. We hate to criticize the solutions of our competitors. And we really hate to do it to Springer & Jacoby's solutions. But we think that the difference between these two slogans is exemplary. One claims emotion, the other triggers it. No doubt about which one we would recommend.

It should be pointed out here that a slogan by no means needs to make sense to thrive. It needs only tonality. Just consider Alles Müller,... oder was? (It's all Müller, ... or what?) The content of this yogurt slogan is more akin to Dadaist Kurt Schwitters than to a well-thought out marketing platform. But the content doesn't matter. Freshness is the message. Or, in the spirit of Marshal McLuhan, "The tonality is the message."

One day, we stumbled upon a Web site with a slogan-writing program, www.sloganizer.de. We were so fascinated that we started a Sixt campaign that consisted entirely of virtual slogans. It was the first campaign generated by a computer. The three slogans that ended up in the campaign were:

"ELEGANCE'S BATTLE CRY OF LOWER PRICES.
THE MOST FASCINATING ESCALATION OF LOWER PRICES.
LOWER PRICES MEAN LOWER PRICES."

CHAPTER 14

IN THE NO MAN'S LAND BETWEEN FEELING AND KNOWING
ABOUT THE RELATIONSHIP BETWEEN AD AGENCY AND CLIENT

Von Matt once told a story about a film he had seen the night before. He had actually only seen the beginning because he was so disappointed that he left after half an hour. Jung was speechless. He had also seen "American Beauty" and was enthusiastic. Right away, he described his favorite scenes to von Matt in such a thrilling way that von Matt was inspired to go and try it again that same night. Now he was enthusiastic too.

This example shows how much creativity—the product—depends on sales skills. And how much can be triggered by persuasion.

Communication is a very special business. The client buys something that doesn't exist yet. And no one can say for sure if and when it might bring the intended success. The ad agency has to make a correspondingly high effort in persuasion.

Advertising has to get the consumer to believe what he is told. We have to get the client to do the same. The most convincing argument is a history of proven successes. But those are hard to come by when an agency is just starting out.

SATURN "DAHATMA," CINEMA SPOT 2004:
> OUR FIRST BOLLYWOOD PRODUCTION TO DATE, WITH UP TO 100 DANCERS AT 34 DEGREES CELSIUS IN THE SHADE. THE SLOGAN AT THE CENTER OF THIS SPOT, "GEIZ IST GEIL" (CHEAP IS COOL), HAS BEEN BY FAR THE MOST FAMOUS OF ALL BIG SLOGANS OUR AGENCY HAS CREATED, BUT IT IS ALSO THE MOST CONTROVERSIAL. EVEN OUR FORMER CHANCELLOR GERHARD SCHRÖDER TOOK A SHOT AT IT.

DIRECTOR: SIRAJ JHAVERI
FILM PRODUCTION: RADICAL MEDIA

IN THE NO MAN'S LAND BETWEEN FEELING AND KNOWING

If a company decides on new computer software or a new vehicle fleet management system it is a completely different situation, since such services are pretty much objectifiable. When you purchase communications services you don't know what you're getting until the cat is let out of the bag. You don't even know for sure if it is actually a cat.

> IT MIGHT BE A SLOTH.

How can a client evaluate the most important contribution of a communication service provider when creativity is so hard to objectify? Just try to judge the success of the "Wassup?" Budweiser beer campaign using a checklist. Or try to analyze the slogan Alles Müller …, oder was? The consumer doesn't care about the semantic content of a TV commercial or a slogan. Even if in interviews he never fails to stress that he expects advertising to supply objective, verifiable information. One of the truisms of market research.

Why do things happen in most blockbuster movies that defy any form of logic? People who mutate into apes, insects, or robots. Cars that turn into spaceships. Extraterrestrials who phone home. No one is surprised that the most successful film ever shown in Germany was a fairytale, "The Jungle Book."

And nobody took issue with the most popular children's program on German TV of the past decades, "The Show with the Mouse," lying to all the kids. The mouse is larger than the elephant. People want fantasy, magic, dreams—not just facts, facts, facts.

OR DOES YOUR CHILD PREFER TO GO TO SCHOOL THAN TO THE MOVIES?

"Fact, fact, fact! ... You are to be in all things regulated and governed ... by fact." What a radical twist Charles Dickens could have given his novel Hard Times if a critique of objectivistic thinking had been permitted in the mid-19th century! Just image if "Girl Number Twenty" had answered Mr. Gradgrind: "Sir, facts are like cows! If you look at them hard enough, they generally run away."

With the fate of his fictional characters, Dickens presented the social and emotional problems arising from a governing philosophy that stated that fantasy and ideas were invalid in the light of naked facts. He regarded the technocratic rationality of his era as a threat. 150 years ago, Dickens used his moralistic, pedagogical novel to defend the principle of "humanity" against the predominant rule of exclusively objectivistic thinking. But how do advertisers defend their ideas when they are confronted with the belief that rational insight alone can provide privileged access to the best solution and is therefore pure knowledge?

Walking the tightrope between feeling and calculation is the real challenge in the dialog between clients and ad agencies. Because certain details matter that can only be determined eye-to-eye. And because it is not enough to pass on pure information. Rather, it is important that this information be understood and turned into knowledge.

IN THE NO MAN'S LAND BETWEEN FEELING AND KNOWING

The briefing is the key event of communication and is thus more important than the presentation itself. That is why it should be better attended. But, unfortunately, company executives rarely make time for briefings. And here lurks a billion dollar danger: agencies work in vain for months (but not for free), broadcast dates are postponed, clients fly back and forth, shaking their heads when they reject creative efforts that have obviously been flawed from the outset. If a shoemaker had to work on the wrong task as often as an ad agency, he would have to charge 1,000 euros for putting a new sole on a shoe just to avoid going bankrupt.

THE BIGGEST PROBLEM
OF COMMUNICATION
IS COMMUNICATION.

One of our clients forbids written briefings because all too often they encourage hiding behind an anonymous piece of paper. You have to be able to look your client in the eye to get a reliable idea of what his product or brand needs. And the client has to sense that the agency understands.

What's wrong with a joint briefing for all the competing agencies? Advertisers may be too vain to sit next to one another voluntarily. But, it's better to be in a briefing with the top brand executive than in one-on-one conversations with people who hardly know the top executive.

Even less efficient than briefings with the wrong person are pre-presentations with the wrong person. Before an agency gets permission to give a big presentation, the advertising buyer likes to prevent the catastrophe of losing face by asking the agency for two or three alternatives. Here, the servant tastes what will later be served to the king. And often the flavor gets lost.

An additional difficulty is simulating an advertising idea's momentum using existing images and film material. Campaign proposals remain immaterial for the client until they get produced. Which means until a lot of production money has been spent.

Even when a campaign has been produced, the frightful question remains. How will the recipients perceive the message? Will the campaign reach its predetermined goals? This presupposes a lot of trust on the client's side. Communication services are — in the true sense of the word — entrusted goods.

For years, our agency produced spots for a commercial campaign in which we reduced the time between briefing and broadcast to five hours. The prerequisite for this world record, however, was unusual trust.

At 3 p.m. the agency received the briefing and at 8 p.m. the spot was on the air. How was that possible? Only because the client delegated complete responsibility for production to the agency. And because the agency acted like a trustee. There was no interim vote and no final sign-off. The agency sent the spot directly to the TV station.

The client saw the spot for the first time when it was broadcast. In one out of ten cases, this resulted in an enraged phone call.

NICHT JEDER KANN SICH EINEN ANZUG KAUFEN,
DER WIRKLICH SITZT.

RENÉ LEZARD
leider teuer!

RENÉ LEZARD "SHAR-PEI," PRINT 1995:
HEADLINE: "NOT EVERYONE CAN BUY A SUIT THAT REALLY FITS."
FASHION ADVERTISING ALMOST ALWAYS FOLLOWS THE SAME STANDARDS. YOU SHOW THE FASHION AND YOU SHOW THE MANUFACTURER'S LOGO. HARDLY ANY CAMPAIGN MAKES USE OF THE POSSIBILITIES OF CREATIVE COMMUNICATION. HARDLY ANYONE USES TEXT. THE CAMPAIGN FOR RENE LEZARD WAS A MILESTONE. IN FASHION ADVERTISING. AND "REGRETTABLY EXPENSIVE" BECAME JUNG VON MATT'S MOST PROVOKING SLOGAN.

PHOTOGRAPHER: KAJETAN KANDLER, C/O KIRSTEN ROSCHLAUB

IN THE NO MAN'S LAND BETWEEN FEELING AND KNOWING

But also in a unique campaign that helped to boost Bild's circulation beyond the five-million mark.

The campaign began on 1 May 1995. We were sitting in the studio, editing the first spot of this campaign. On a side monitor, the Grand Prix of San Marino was showing, something von Matt didn't want to miss. Suddenly, the accident occurred in which Ayrton Senna died. We spontaneously decided to make his death the topic of a new spot, which we produced within half an hour. It was not possible to vote on this change. The agency felt secure enough to bear this responsibility and had the spot broadcast.

Speaking of death. On 1 February 2001, German chanteuse Hildegard Knef died and we had a heartfelt TV spot ready to go that promised an in-depth pictorial about her last days. The macabre twist to this story was that the spot had been ready for years because we had produced it on an earlier occasion when Mrs. Knef was not doing well.

Dear Reader, if you happen to be a celebrity and have been very sick at some point, please excuse us for having your feature spot ready on the shelf.

IT IS THE NATURE OF OUR BUSINESS
THAT FINAL RESULTS MIGHT DIFFER FROM
THE AGREED-UPON PLAN.

One of our most fascinating commercials was only created because the client trusted us and stayed cool. This was the first commercial film for the fashion designer René Lezard. We presented a script as usual. The client agreed.

Then we went looking for a suitable director and found Mehdi Norowzian, an Iranian living in London. We asked him to write down his interpretation of the script but he wrote a completely new one. We presented it to our client, who—lacking experience—considered it normal that a film script could take a 180° turn in a matter of days. He agreed again.

The film Mehdi produced had nothing to do with either script number one or script number two. With the worst conscience a trustee could ever have, Deneke von Weltzien got on a train to meet with people from René Lezard. Again, the client agreed and, in turn, got a piece of advertising with high momentum.

In a creativity-oriented agency it cannot always be assured that the final recommendation corresponds exactly to the initial elaborate strategy. If we find a campaign in the vicinity of the strategy that is much more fascinating than our so-called "right" campaign we tend to recommend

> THE MORE ENCHANTING ROUTE
> OFF THE BEATEN PATH.

Not, however, without communicating the detour.

This goes along with our deep conviction that excellent ideas are not only perishable goods but are also quite rare. And that the momentum of a great idea can more than balance the strategic imperfection. Now more than ever, advertising must be as right as necessary and as fascinating as possible. And not the other way around.

Any client with a long-term vision will always understand if an agency fights for such a position. Unfortunately, ideas are often not valued highly, which can result in uninhibited critiquing of creative work and dismissing the creative team's defensiveness as divaesque bitchiness, vanity, and hypersensitivity.

In such cases Jung usually calms down his fellow defenders by saying, "No agency has ever been fired because they were stubborn. Only because they were sloppy." One of our clients, who is well acquainted with our stubbornness, readily admitted, "Better to have a horse that you have to rein in than one that needs to be kicked all the time."

How far should an agency try to guess what the client is thinking? In this matter we adopt the theory of naiveté. Advertising advisors, especially creative people, should be able to approach their tasks unburdened by excessive knowledge and internal details.

Because too much knowledge distances them from their target audience—the consumer—who they need to emulate. If extensive insider knowledge were actually useful, there would be more examples of companies who successfully create their communications concepts in-house.

We also don't believe that an ad agency has to have sector experience to deliver good work. Of course it should have the same awareness level as the intended target group, but not necessarily more than that.

We will never forget the moment when Jung was in the middle of praising our special competence in the Wining and Dining department to Mövenpick's management. Suddenly, a stream of water squirted across the conference room and soaked the entire executive team. Von Matt could not have opened that mineral water bottle any less clumsily, but we still won the account.

Another insight for an optimal partnership. An ad agency has to break free from all the hierarchical structures of the client's enterprise if it wants to maintain advisory and inspirational competence. Otherwise, every agency recommendation will be examined for its tactical quality from the get-go. "If Mr. A likes this, Ms. B won't accept it."

There seem to be two kinds of advertising advisors. One who concentrates his entire career on his craft, i.e., finding communication solutions. The client's enterprise is of little interest to him. The other one—bored with the repetitive tasks in communication—aspires to become an economic advisor. The actual advertising is of little interest to him. Both positions are less than optimal.

IN COMMUNICATION, THE BIG PICTURE IS IMPORTANT.
SO ARE THE DETAILS.

BENSON & HEDGES "MATCH," BILLBOARD 1994:
HEADLINE: "BURNED. BUT HAPPY."
NOTHING IS MORE GENERIC FOR CIGARETTE ADS THAN TO SHOW A PACK AND PRAISE THE PLEASURES OF SMOKING. FOR BENSON & HEDGES WE WENT A DIFFERENT WAY AND HIGH ATTENTION VALUES PROVED US RIGHT. HOWEVER, WE COULDN'T PUSH THROUGH OUR FAVORITE HEADLINE, WHICH READ: IT DIED FOR A GOOD CAUSE.

PHOTOGRAPHER: UWE DÜTTMANN

IN THE NO MAN'S LAND BETWEEN FEELING AND KNOWING

All too often we witness terrible communication that was based on a great entrepreneurial vision.

We have noticed that the roles of ad agency and client have reversed themselves. In the pioneering days of advertising, the client knew all about the entrepreneurial aspect and saw the advertising specialist as the resourceful mediator of his sales message. Today we are often faced with the following paradoxical situation.

The agency dives deep into marketing analyses and tries to lecture the client in his own field of expertise. The client, on the other hand, tries to direct the creative aspect to the last detail as if he had studied it. He rewrites copy, dictates design changes, and drives everyone crazy with directions during the shooting of the commercial. A foreboding form of job rotation.

Just as if the European Union organized a big party and distributed the responsibilities like this: the Spanish organize, the English do the cooking, the French check the tickets at the door, the Germans take care of the entertainment, AND THE GREEKS ARE IN CHARGE OF THE EQUIPMENT.

The results of the reversed roles are the TV commercials we enjoy every day. The viewer at home might think that they were created by advertising experts. The truth is, they were not created by advertising experts but by misprogrammed product managers.

These interface problems are naturally at their most extreme when an ad agency works for a creative sector. Fashion houses, for example, often tend to assume, "If I can knit pullovers,

I can knit advertising as well." The more creative the ad agency, the more difficult the struggle with creative clients.

Again and again, companies approach us and demand a "Sixt campaign." Because they know the success of those ads and are reminded of it at every airport. One long briefing discussion ended with the sentence "Just do something like the stuff you did for Sixt and the account is yours."

And even though we had the same team work on it, the team who had thought up some excellent Sixt advertising just the day before, it became clear that such a communication success was only possible with an exceptional client like Sixt. A client who believes in communication and personally tends to every campaign instead of adding fabric softener by committee. Advertising that has to be approved by committees or even by a few different parties will probably be ground to dust in the mills of dialecticism.

CONSENSUS AND NONSENSE ARE OFTEN NOT THAT FAR FROM EACH OTHER.

Thesis and antithesis result in synthesis. Communications tasks in particular are not constructed in such a way that they can be solved by compromise. That's the reason why no committee has ever been honored with a monument.

Committees are often so busy dealing with themselves that the presence of external communication experts turns a presentation into a farce. Even more inefficient are meetings where the most important source of ideas — the ad agency — has not been invited. It's as if patients in a hospital locked the doors to their rooms from the inside and started to heal each other.

The frequently incalculable business of communication, with its many possibilities for misunderstanding, requires hand-to-hand combat. The direct, intense dialog between the main characters without the usual crowd of extras. This hand-to-hand combat is the prerequisite for successful communication.

So, what else can a client do to get better results? First, he has to buy at the right time, like a stock trader. Generally, the creative process is shaped like a curve that first rises steeply, then it reaches its peak, and then suffers a sharp decline. This means that the creative teams usually reach their "peak of excellence" after a certain warm-up phase, then become weaker by small increments until they run out of steam and interest.

This is similar to the situation where an actor has to say the same sentence thirty times. His seventh try will probably be better than his first. But his thirtieth will probably be weaker than his seventh. The same goes for athletes in track and field. Bad advertising often happens because the client is too late in saying

"BINGO"

without noticing that the creative energy has long since faded. (Admittedly, a Bingo that's too early is not ideal either.)

The client should also be willing to accept that his advertising sometimes works better and sometimes worse. But this willingness is rare. In the first year he waits patiently, in the second year nervously, for his outstanding communication success. And as soon as he gets it, he tries to standardize it. He looks for the features of Super Success Part I, deduces criteria for Super Success Part II, and drives the creative team crazy. Especially if Super Success Part II is delayed until the third year.

MOMENTUM CANNOT BE PROGRAMMED.

If you are able to tell your client that the Lord only helps those who are relaxed, you are not far from being a damned good trustee.

The Japanese emperor Katsura wanted to enlist the architect Koboti Enshu to construct his palace. The architect posed three demands. 1. It takes as long as it takes. 2. It costs at much as it costs. And 3. The emperor is only allowed to see it when it is finished. After 46 years of construction, Enshu finished building one of the most beautiful palaces in the world. The total cost has never been reported.

Let's remain modest and restrict our demands to the third request. The client is only allowed to see the advertising when it is finished. He stays out of all decisions in the meantime. What a gain in time and quality!

The same thing that leads a downhill skier to win his medal also leads an ad agency's client to success. Determining the right direction, letting his skis run while being alert and able to correct his path in precarious situations, and trying to make himself as small as possible. A mindset that is far too rare in practice.

Insecure clients can turn a downhill ski course into a slalom by constantly correcting the direction and slowing down the run. If someone interrupts every scene in the tense, concentrated atmosphere of a film shoot, moping about details, it hurts the results. That person makes the team insecure and drains its energy.

40 years ago, von Matt had a pivotal experience in this respect. For the first time, he was able to afford a hairdresser-to-the-stars, Göpf Möri in Zurich. Just as Möri started to cut, von Matt corrected him. And then again and again, about every three minutes. Mr. Möri's mood took a nosedive and the end result was a life lesson, embossed on von Matt's head.

Of course, advertisers make mistakes. And those who want to drive advertising effect to its limits make more than others. We have also created our share of flops, campaigns that didn't have the desired success or that backfired. But why do we advertisers always have such a hard time admitting to our mistakes? Why do we have to whitewash everything in the end?

When we started with the daily TV commercials for Bild, we were fully aware that we couldn't vouch for consistent quality with five hours between briefing and broadcast. Since the tight timing made it impossible to show the finished spot to the client before it went on the air, we became insecure.

We went to the Editor-in-Chief and explained that we couldn't guarantee that every spot would be top quality. He gave a simple answer. "I can't guarantee that my newspaper is top quality every day either."

One of the most unforgettable moments in von Matt's career happened when a Ferrero executive informed him that his campaign had not set anything in motion. Unforgettable most of all because of the last sentence and the Italian accent in which it was uttered:

> WE WROTE A LETTER TO THE CONSUMER
> BUT IT GOT LOST IN THE MAIL.

Usually, the worst-case scenario in advertising is when the spot has no positive effect. We only experience negative effects on very rare occasions. Once with Sixt. We were supposed to create an ad that announced Sixt's leasing offer loud and clear. As always, we wanted maximum momentum. It was Mr. Sixt's opinion that the entire industry pays too much for their vehicle fleets and he wanted to get that point across to Germany's chief buyers.

Our idea was not to place a normal ad but to publish a list. Headline: "Here is a list of all the companies who pay too much for their vehicle fleet." On the list were Germany's 500 biggest companies, basically all potential customers for Sixt Leasing. The ad caused an uproar because it was taken literally, against all expectations.

Germany's executives assumed that the list in the Sixt ad had been researched properly and, as a result, confronted their buyers and fleet managers. They felt that it hurt their reputation that they had been publicly denounced as "cash burners." At some point, the Sixt company wrote 500 letters of apology. A big headache, although in the end it was also a big plug for Sixt's competitive leasing offer.

After all, marketing communication follows the same principle as the one stated by Formula One World Champion Mario Andretti — and nobody has put it better:

> **"IF THINGS SEEM UNDER CONTROL**
> YOU'RE JUST NOT GOING FAST ENOUGH."

CHAPTER 15

BOREDOM HAS NEVER BEEN AS DEADLY AS TODAY
ABOUT COMMUNICATION IN THE DIGITAL WORLD

The media landscape and media use have fundamentally changed—and will continue to change, with new end-user devices, the mobile Internet, and applications in every-day items ("Internet of Things").

Today, people use mass media not as a fixed agenda item in their day planner but rather more situation-bound and intertwined with their daily lives. Our prognosis that media use is becoming more voluntary has become reality.

Although television still remains an important, far-reaching medium, the tendency is clear: every individual creates his or her own information and entertainment program. Will advertising interruptions, even as pre-roll or post-roll ads, still have a chance to survive? We shall see.

What is clear is this: if there are more ways to avoid bad advertising, we need better ideas.

In one of his presentations, Jung developed the following image as the new challenge for marketing communication: if we assume that advertising is basically "playing catch" with the consumers because it wants to touch them and they would rather avoid this contact, then we have been playing this game on a meadow until now. Everybody knew were the others were. "Reach" was the topic. With a large advertising budget, it was possible to wear out anyone who was on the run and finally catch up. Totally didn't matter what the advertisement looked like.

Today, we are playing this game in a forest, where the consumers have new possibilities to hide from us, but we also have new opportunities to surprise them.

> THE GAME HAS THUS BECOME MORE VARIED AND SOPHISTICATED.

By new forms of advertisement, by ambient installations, by product placement, by in-game advertising, by branded content, the combination of brand messages with editorial content, or branded entertainment.

Or by sophisticated e-mail accounts that scan and analyze word contents and accordingly infuse advertising messages. And by the many opportunities that the social media, such as blogs, Facebook, Twitter, video portals, etc., have to offer.

Or even by advertising that no longer functions according to the sender-receiver principle, but where brands launch products and invite their target groups to participate.

The reasons why people devote their time and attention to brands at all, why they communicate with and about brands, companies and consumption have remained the same: group identity, self-promotion, and self-affirmation—and sometimes simply boredom, or, more positively put: the expectation of being entertained. Not just as a passive audience but as active participants.

But the ways and situations how and where people deal with brands, products and companies have fundamentally changed over the past decade. The Internet has more rapidly evolved into a mass medium than we anticipated ten years ago. The mobile Internet is growing at a similarly rapid pace.

In view of the increasingly shorter innovation cycles in communications technology, the current status quo is really nothing more than a snapshot. Therefore, it makes very little sense to deal with single media and current innovations.

We are dealing with the big picture: which new basic requirements does the digitalized world of communication have for advertising agencies and their customers?

FROM OUR POINT OF VIEW, THERE ARE FOUR:
1. Which media and communication channels are used and how they are used must be part of the creative concept. Ten years ago, the creative use of media was a rarely used opportunity (see chapter 12). Today and in the future, it is simply the requirement for reach and awareness in the correct target group. It does not just involve the choice of a channel we can use to send messages. Creative use of media must also be understood as creative use of technologies as well as forms and situations of communication.

IS THE CHANNEL FOR THRILLERS, HORROR AND CRIME.

13TH STREET "LAST CALL," INTERACTIVE CINEMA SPOT 2010: "LAST CALL" SHOWS A YOUNG WOMAN ESCAPING FROM AN OLD SANATORIUM. WE ASKED THE MOVIEGOERS BEFORE THE SHOW TO SEND THEIR PHONE NUMBER TO A SPEED DIAL NUMBER. DURING HER ESCAPE, THE LEAD ACTRESS CALLS ONE OF THE AUDIENCE MEMBERS IN ORDER TO HELP SAVE HER FROM A DANGEROUS MAN IN HER PURSUIT. SPECIALLY DESIGNED VOICE RECOGNITION SOFTWARE ENABLED THIS VERY REALISTIC DIALOGUE BETWEEN MOVIE CHARACTER AND VIEWER.

DIRECTOR: MILO
FILM PRODUCTION: FILM DELUXE
SOFTWARE: POWERFLASHER GMBH

2. Today, an R&D budget, even for marketing communication, is more necessary than ever before. Those who always wait until new forms of communication have proven to be effective and can be assessed according to existing guidelines will miss out on many opportunities. For many years, with our initiative "10% in search of excellence," we have pleaded for the idea to test innovative forms even in communications with a fixed budget in order to collect valuable experiences.

3. Advertising as we see it aims to conquer. There are better tools for customer retention (see chapter 2). But nowadays, when social networks have the same reach as mass media, one's own customer base becomes an important player in the communications game—for better or for worse.

Brands have to learn how to deal with criticism. But what's much more important: we can and must integrate the power of the networks, the knowledge and ideas of the crowd into our work. Brands are welcome when they appear with an open mind, not as condescending high-school teachers.

4. Consistency and attitude without stubbornness and formalisms are necessary to remain recognizable as a brand personality. Because it can happen at any time that companies are severely criticized publicly—and then immediately have to decide whether to issue a change or explain themselves, stand by their decision and weather the criticism. Many marketing decision-makers have already learned that they cannot continue with their regular approval processes if they want to react quickly enough.

How do brands get attention in a fragmented, digitalized media landscape? What is creativity if the smart headline, the fascinating image idea, the exciting advertising spot only represent fitting solutions for part of the job? What will happen to that one idea which, up to now, has been responsible for momentum?

The ingenious spot that turned something around in the consumer's head or the effective poster people see in passing will continue to be important elements in advertising. But people are willing to devote much more time if brands make intelligent or even entertaining offers and take the consumers seriously as participants in the game. This is where the digital media offer many, always innovative, opportunities.

It is still important which core values and what attitude people are supposed to connect with a brand. But the brand is no longer required to communicate this with over-the-top intensity. Many of the media used by consumers today no longer offer a suitable format for advertising in the traditional sense.

IT'S NOT A BUG, IT'S A FEATURE!

This type of solution requires teams where a wide variety of creative talents and specialists collaborate. Now more than ever before we have to deal with our target groups, and imagine their lives, their daily processes, their abilities and passions. And then, at the right opportunity and in the best possible manner, introduce our brand, our product, our message, our agenda into the game. As a highly welcome but not entirely altruistic present—as a Trojan horse.

BOREDOM HAS NEVER BEEN AS DEADLY AS TODAY

To construct such horses, we need more expertise than ever before: technological know-how, product and brand knowledge, consumer insights beyond abstract desires and attitudes, and, of course, creativity. This is where people who, until now, rather happily avoided one another because they thought the others were uncool or crazy, must work closely together with mutual respect.

Many of the more recent ideas from our agency group would not have seen the light of day without this close collaboration.

One example is a digital idea for the World Wildlife Fund organization that garnered global attention: The goal was to protect the tree population from unnecessary paper use. Thus we invented the "WWF" as a non-printable version of the PDF file format and spread the idea with the slogan "Save as WWF, save a tree."

Or the unique "Last Call" for the TV network "13th Street," where, for the first time, the movie audience had a hand in determining the plot of a thriller. The audience members had provided their cell phone numbers before the showing so that the actors could call them in the middle of the movie and ask them for advice. Suddenly, they became part of the action and shared intense responsibility for the fate of the character. "Last Call" demonstrated very impressively how fundamental the difference between "audience and recipient of a message" and "participant and co-creator" could be. The digital world does not only allow us to entrust our target groups with an active and central role—the invitation to participate is often the requirement to awaken their interest at all.

By skillful early use of a digital innovation, our Stuttgart agency landed a coup that made a big impact in the industry. When "Facebook" started its new function "Places" in Germany, nobody had any idea that our guys had manipulated it a month earlier for a guerilla-type recruiting campaign.

We simply set up our competitors' locations ahead of time for ourselves, so that everybody who checked in there with a mobile device via "Facebook Places" was greeted by us: "Winner! Would you like to be one too? Then why don't you check in at www.jvm-neckar.de/jobs—we are looking for new talent!"

With so much innovation, so many untested waters, one has to have courage to experiment. But we have also noticed that marketing has increasingly been under surveillance by the controllers.

Which makes sense to a degree, since companies invest in their communications department more than ever before. But even in the digital age, dependable proof of effectiveness still remains a challenge: there are too many factors in the game.

Despite the direct metrics provided by digital media, this has not changed. People generally see more than just the banner, which eventually leads them to the order form. (Which in turn leads to more sophisticated tracking concepts by the online media marketers and advertisers. And also creates deeper wrinkles on the foreheads of worried data privacy advocates.) Much more importantly: How much worth is the time people invest in a project that brands have initiated? What is the value when people get involved, create something themselves and activate their personal network?

BOREDOM HAS NEVER BEEN AS DEADLY AS TODAY

Below the bottom line, the digital world does make it easier for us to check the effects of communications measures with limited financial risk. But in our view, there are still not enough marketing decision-makers who are really interested in understanding the effects of their activities.

Maybe not quite without reason. Because marketing, with its high degree of individual decisions based on personal taste and the inherent, rather thin evidence of effectiveness, has always been a thorn in the side of colleagues who, in their professional environment, are measured by hard facts such as sales figures or the product's performance values. And every failure was gleefully used as a fundamental criticism of marketing.

A steady R&D budget would raise the error tolerance for marketing and ensure faster and less painful learning effects.

Especially since brands nowadays have their own online media that can be used for test projects: their own home page, online service platforms for their customer base, newsletters, apps. The so-called "owned media."

And we can add to that another channel, the "earned media": the reach earned by a brand through the attractiveness of its digital offerings. The more innovative and interesting these offerings are, the larger their spread in personal networks will be.

We all have learned by now that viral networking is no reliable recipe for "high media performance without financial input." The actual attractiveness of a communications offer or a project idea is simply very hard to estimate ahead of time. Just like any music mogul could not predict without fail: "this will be a number-one hit."

But experiments and "test balloons" are not concerned with extended reach anyway. And exceptions always confirm the rule.

Up to now, the greatest viral success in the history of our agency was the Sixt vacation rental car campaign with German pop singer Matthias Reim. Even the feature article about the campaign at Bild.de received over 2 million clicks.

Reim was known as a bankrupt has-been, after he had to declare bankruptcy a few years ago within a huge media storm. We were able to convince him to re-record his greatest, and also only, hit "Verdammt, ich lieb Dich—ich lieb Dich nicht" (Damn, I love you—I don't love you") with the refrain: "Verdammt ich hab nix—ich miet bei Sixt" (Damn, I ain't got zilch—I'll rent with Sixt). The song's video was the core of a campaign that basically spread on its own without any media expenses, and still continues to spread to this day via YouTube.

For us, advertising means conquering. But, at least in mature markets in Central Europe and in most Western countries, growth is only possible by displacement. The tougher the competition, the more expensive each new customer becomes.

It seems to make much more sense to invest in retaining the customer base and to grow with new offers for current customers. The hype about CRM at the end of the last millennium

WWF "SAVE AS WWF, SAVE A TREE," SOFTWARE 2010:
AS A CONTRIBUTION OF THE ENVIRONMENTAL PROTECTION AGENCY "WORLD WILDLIFE FUND" AGAINST UNNECESSARY PAPER USE, WE INVENTED "THE WWF," A FILE FORMAT THAT CAN BE OPENED, FORWARDED AND SAVED—BUT NOT PRINTED. A BRILLIANTLY SIMPLE IDEA THAT FOUND ACCEPTANCE VIA TWITTER, BLOGS AND NETWORKS IN 195 COUNTRIES.

MERCEDES-BENZ "TRAMP A BENZ," SOCIAL MEDIA 2010:
WHEN STREET PHOTOGRAPHER STEFAN GBURECK STARTED OUT ON HIS JOURNEY IN DECEMBER 2010, IT DID NOT MATTER WHERE HE WAS HEADED. BUT HOW HE GOT THERE. WHICH WAS ONLY BY MERCEDES-BENZ. THE GOAL: THE STRICTEST INTERPRETATION OF GOTTLIEB DAIMLER'S MOTTO: THE BEST OR NOTHING. THE EXTERNAL CONDITIONS: ONE OF THE COLDEST WINTERS GERMANY HAD EVER EXPERIENCED. AND THE INCERTITUDE: WOULD STEFAN FIND ENOUGH MERCEDES-BENZ DRIVERS TO TAKE HIM TO WARMER CLIMATES? BUT HE DID NOT GET DISAPPOINTED. STEFAN BLOGGED ABOUT HIS EXPERIENCES WHENEVER POSSIBLE. AFTER JUST A SHORT WHILE, MORE AND MORE PEOPLE DISCUSSED "THE BEST OR NOTHING" AND THE IDEA BEHIND IT. THE COMBINATION OF ART, SOCIAL MEDIA AND ADVERTISING. THE BUZZ GENERATED BY THIS INITIATIVE WAS IMMENSE. PLEASANT SIDE EFFECT: PHOTOS, VIDEOS AND STORIES ABOUT THE DECISION FOR A MERCEDES-BENZ, WHICH YIELDED AN EXHIBITION, PRESENTATIONS AND—A VERY CLASSIC RESULT—A BOOK.

PHOTOGRAPHER: STEFAN GBURECK

was the reaction to this insight. In the meantime, customer retention is as much part of marketing as digital elements in an advertising campaign.

Even companies who distribute their products via retail channels have the opportunity to get to know their customers: through service offers on their own home page or their own brand presence in social networks. The customer base and brand loyalists can be identified much more easily and hence be addressed much more directly than before.

When we accepted the account for the Internet provider 1&1, the brand had two identities: it was highly innovative but their service performance was perceived as far below average. The Web was full of opinions from unsatisfied customers.

The challenge was immense. And we knew that a new ad campaign alone would not solve the problem—we basically had to restart the brand. Concrete actions were required.

We recommended to make service the main topic and named an authentic, long-term employee "the Customer Satisfaction Manager." He became the face of the brand, internally and externally, and he also received the necessary funds to make changes.

At first, the consumers reacted with skepticism: Is this guy real? Or just an advertising gimmick?

Social media helped us prove his validity: after five million responses to customer inquiries and e-mails, six significant innovations, and two blogger meetings, all doubts were silenced: the guy was real, and his customers were so dear to him that he received over 26 marriage proposals in the first year alone – in digital form, of course.

No wonder that 1&1 is now seen as customer-friendly and gets recommended to others more than ever before.

The good old adage "customers recruit customers" now gains a whole new dimension. The so-called "earned media" have developed into real mass media. But—as the name suggests—a brand must first earn this success: only satisfied customers recommend offers and products to others. And the give and take must be balanced.

The more creatively and attractively a brand rewards its customer base for loyalty and word-of-mouth propaganda, the more unmistakable the relationship between customer and brand will become. Advertising, customer maintenance and service offers are more closely intertwined than ever before: Brave New World. Much more complex than the world of ad campaigns that shaped the early years of Jung von Matt—but also more multi-faceted.

The example of 1&1 also shows that advertisers and marketing people must get used to a different way of working. We cannot devote our efforts and energy to campaigns with time limits. Projects, for which we have successfully recruited enthusiastic co-warriors, cannot simply be "turned off" when the campaign is over. We have to work with a much more lasting effect, with more editorial input, more spontaneity and flexibility.

BOREDOM HAS NEVER BEEN AS DEADLY AS TODAY

Von Matt doubts that he would still be motivated after almost 40 years of creative battles at the advertising front if the playing field "communication" had not changed. The media revolution sparked a new ambition in him for at least another decade. But of course, the power of the social networks also has its downside: each company must take into account that it will get criticized, that viral campaigns can also be directed against its own brand or its own product.

Lies, false representation of facts, whitewashing and beating around the bush, even the legally validated, corporate-language compatible advertising slogans disguised as the authentic reaction of an employee in a discussion—all this will be quickly unmasked on the Web. And much more consistently so, if a company increasingly tries to use social networks and communities for its own purposes.

People invest themselves in brands because they believe they are doing the right thing and can improve their status in the community. They also have a lot to lose if it turns out that the brand has cheated them. That's when amateur bloggers react in the same way as the journalist who must realize that the press secretary's exclusive information was not exclusive at all, or that he was used as a tool for concealed advertising.

If the wind blows in your direction, you need steadfastness, even as a brand. It's true: nowadays, brands have much less control over who talks about them in what way. That's why it is good to stand behind what one does, even if not everybody agrees with it.

BOREDOM HAS NEVER BEEN AS DEADLY AS TODAY

When von Matt once wrote a note to all of his employees in a slightly overemotional tone, something happened that can happen very easily in the digital world: it became public. And since his message contained an absolutely electrifying critique of blogs—he called them "the toilet walls of the Internet"—, he felt the concentrated rage and power of this media type. His word coinage was translated into more than 20 languages and spread worldwide. Even the New York Times quoted his "toilet wall."

After conferring with a few industry colleagues, von Matt decided to send an explanation to the blogger who kicked off this affair. And this too spread like wildfire, but at least its content calmed many tempers in the blogosphere.

In view of the power of the social networks it is often said that the brand no longer belongs to the company alone; that its power to guide and control the brand is dwindling. This is correct. And it is also incorrect.

Correct is that hollow brand promises that are neither backed up by performance or attitude will be exposed more quickly. We like that. The loss of control also entails that fans make use of parts of the Corporate Design—unauthorized, of course, and completely different from what the CD manual prescribes.

This certainly angers our designers who came up with a good reason behind every single rule. But first of all the brand should be happy about the high involvement—and think hard about playing the "brand copyright" card.

BOREDOM HAS NEVER BEEN AS DEADLY AS TODAY

Celebrities are celebrities because they do not belong to themselves alone but because their fans make them their own. Even if it can be a pain sometimes, and they get embarrassed by their own fans. But it would be worse if they no longer turned any heads. And exactly that is unlikely to happen to von Matt after his toilet wall affair.

And as far as the question of power is concerned: brands that also take a position in social networks and defend their decisions keep control of the steering wheel.

This can sometimes lead to losing a few customers who had a different idea about the brand. But they will also gain some others. The digitalization of our lives has changed many things. But it also didn't change many others. Advertising requires a certain fighting spirit:

SCRATCHES ARE SEXY.
THE SWEAT OF FEAR IS NOT.

WITHOUT THESE PEOPLE, OUR BOOK WOULD HAVE REMAINED A COLLECTION OF SCRIBBLES ON PAPER:

Giovanni Castell, the photographer of our title picture. He's from our neighborhood. One day he called and asked us if he could take our picture. It would be quick. We went down to the courtyard, and we got the most unusual picture taken of us so far.

Deike Leiner and Biljana Retzlik, the two best whiners and nudgers among our long-term professional companions. They managed to get us to sit at a table and make us deliver one hundred and sixty pages each, on time.

Götz Ulmer and Julia Ulmer, who designed the book. And never lost courage in the tug-of-war between "this book should be unusual" and "this book should be a totally normal and easy read."

A book written by advertisers will always remain half-knowledge. André Schulz, our scientific collaborator, assured with his contributions and meticulous research that it isn't only quarter-knowledge.